Armageddon: The Devil's Payday

Marvin Moore

Pacific Presss Publishing Association
Boise, Idaho
Oshawa, Ontario, Canada

Edited by David C. Jarnes
Cover design by Mark Winchester
Inside design by Patrick McCoy
Typeset in 10/11 Times Roman

Unless otherwise noted, all Scripture quotations are taken from
the New International Version. Also, all emphasis supplied in
the Scripture quoted is the author's.

Library of Congress Cataloging-in-Publication Data:
Moore, Marvin, 1937-
    Armageddon: The Devil's Payday / Marvin Moore.
        p.   cm.
    Includes bibliographical references.
    ISBN 0-8163-1318-0 (Pbk.)
    1. Eschatology—Biblical teaching. 2. Bible—Prophecies—
Eschatology. 3. Bible. N.T. Revelation—Criticism, interpreta-
tion, etc. 4. Second Advent. 5. Christian life—Seventh-day Ad-
ventist authors. 6. Seventh-day Adventists—Doctrines.
1. Title.
BT821.2.M659   1995
236'.9—dc20   95-42093
                                                          CIP

95 96 97 98 99 ● 5 4 3 2 1

Contents

Preface

Revelation is a book about the end time—the months and years leading up to the second coming of Christ and the millennium that follows. Revelation tells us that earth's history will climax in a terrible struggle between the forces of good and evil, a battle for control of our planet. All the people who live on earth will be drawn into this conflict; regrettably, most of them on the side of God's enemy—the side that ultimately will be defeated.

The book you're holding in your hands will take you through Revelation, identifying its themes and warnings and laying out the spiritual choices you and I will have to make during earth's final days to be on the winning side, to remain loyal to God in this war.

While the book is new, the chapters in it are not. When I became the editor of *Signs of the Times* in August 1994, I decided that during 1995 I would write one article a month on the biblical book of Revelation. My article in the January issue, "Armageddon: The Devil's Payday," is the first chapter of this book, and the fourteen chapters that follow come from subsequent issues of *Signs*.

Revelation's depiction of the end time shows a definite chronological sequence at certain points. With one exception, you will find that the chapters of this book in which chronology is important have been put in proper sequence. The exception is "Armageddon: The Devil's Payday." Although it appears first in the book, chronologically, it belongs between chapters 9 and 10.

Perhaps I should mention something else that you're likely to notice as you read this book: It's written a little differently than what you might expect. The reason is simply that writing a series of articles for a magazine differs from writing the same number of chapters for a book.

Book authors can assume that most readers will start at the beginning and go straight through. Consequently, they don't need to repeat later in their books what they say in their beginning—at least not much repetition will be required. Magazine authors, on the other hand, have to assume that some readers will first pick up the magazines halfway through the series. So they need to give enough background information in each article that new readers can make sense of what they're saying. This, of course, means that readers who have followed the series from the beginning will get a certain amount of repetition in later issues of the magazine.

In making the *Signs* articles into a book, I decided to retain essentially the same wording as appeared in the magazine. As you read this book, then, you will notice some repetition. I hope that despite this repetition, the spiritual message of Revelation shines through to you from these pages and that when you have finished the book you will understand God, His Son Jesus, and the way to eternal life better than when you started!

David Jarnes, my associate editor at *Signs of the Times*, especially deserves a big thank-you for his contribution to this book. During the year that I have been editor of *Signs*, I have come to really appreciate his skill as an editor. David edited each article as it appeared in the magazines during 1995 and early 1996, and he also fine-tuned the editing as we made the articles into a book. Thanks to David's professional touch, these articles, and now the book, are much more readable.

Marvin Moore

chapter one

Armageddon: The Devil's Payday

The morning of January 16, 1991, I was attending a class on the biblical doctrine of end-time events when the news broke that United Nations forces had attacked Iraq. The professor cancelled the afternoon session. The rest of that day and on into the next, we kept our eyes riveted on our television sets.

Fifty days later, Saddam Hussein's troops hunkered in underground bunkers as Allied aircraft pounded them with a hail of bombs. The petrified Iraqi soldiers defected to the Allies in droves.

The Gulf War was very real to those of us who saw it on our television sets. But it was a thousand times more real to those who experienced it.

I have bad news for you. Another war is just around the corner, and it's going to make Desert Storm seem like a kid's game of cowboys and Indians. Revelation calls this coming war Armageddon. Fortunately, we haven't been left in the dark—Revelation has a lot to say about this war. Let's look at a few of its more descriptive verses:

• The dragon was enraged at the woman and went off to make war against the rest of her offspring (chapter 12:17).
• I saw a beast coming out of the sea. . . . He was given power to make war against the saints and to conquer them (chapter 13:1, 7).

• I saw a woman sitting on a scarlet beast that was covered with blasphemous names and had seven heads and ten horns. . . . The ten horns . . . are ten kings. . . . They will make war against the Lamb (chapter 17:3, 12, 14).

• Then I saw the beast and the kings of the earth and their armies gathered together to make war against the rider on the horse and his army (chapter 19:19).

This war actually began in heaven thousands of years ago when Satan, also called the devil, rebelled against God. A third of the angels sided with him, and because of their rebellion, the devil and these followers of his were expelled from heaven and cast into the earth (verse 9). The devil's conflict against God has continued on our planet ever since.

Armageddon will simply be the end-time battle of that war, when the devil will learn all about the consequences of rebelling against God.

Right now this war doesn't seem real, does it?—you and I "chatting" about it in the same detached sort of way we talk about Rome's conquest of Greece two thousand years ago. But the conflict between Greece and Rome is history. No one will ever feel the terror of that war again. Armageddon, on the other hand, is future—and I believe it's very near. You and I are staring the devil eyeball to bloodshot eyeball, and he's belching his sulfurous breath in our nostrils.

I don't want to terrify you, but I hope you'll get emotional enough about Armageddon that you'll want to know more about it. I'd like to go back over those descriptions we just read from Revelation and analyze them one at a time with you. Let's see what we can learn about this end-time battle. Who will be the main participants?

War with the dragon

"The dragon was enraged at the woman and went off to make war against the rest of her offspring" (Revelation 12:17).

What or who is this dragon? Who is the "woman" he's attacking? And who are her offspring?

Revelation tells us exactly who the parties in this conflict are. We've already learned that the dragon is Satan—the devil. The woman and her offspring represent "those who obey God's commandments and hold to the testimony of Jesus" (verse 17). Those are God's people—Christians, if you please!

War with the sea beast

Immediately after John's report about the dragon's attack on the woman, he introduces us to a powerful creature that stalks out of the ocean: "I saw a beast coming out of the sea," he says. "He had ten horns and seven heads, with ten crowns on his horns, and on each head a blasphemous name" (Revelation 13:1).

Picture it, if you will—this monster with seven heads, each with a blasphemous name burned into its forehead. It stamps its way across the beach, water pouring off its back and running in rivulets back into the ocean.

What on earth is this beast?

For one thing, it is very powerful. People all over the world will follow it, and they will ask, "Who is like the beast? Who can make war against him?" (verse 4). This beast is invincible! Nobody can attack him and win.

Yet a few courageous people do try. Revelation says this beast was "given power to make war against the saints and to conquer them" (verse 7). The saints—that's God's people again—will resist this beast. They will pay a heavy price for their resistance, though. Revelation says that the beast will *conquer* the saints. God's people are doomed!

Or are they?

War with the scarlet beast

The next reference to Armageddon comes in Revelation 17. This chapter opens with a word picture of a prostitute riding on a scarlet beast that, like the beast in chapter 13, has seven heads and ten horns.

The reference to war comes in verse 14, which says, "*They* will make war against the Lamb."

"They" refers to the ten horns on the scarlet beast, and verse 12 explains that these horns represent ten kings. *Kings* means "heads of state," which in our day can include presidents and prime ministers. In the broadest sense, these kings represent the nations over which they rule. There are far more than ten nations in the world today. Revelation's "ten kings" should probably be understood to represent all the nations of the world at the time of this final conflict.[1]

Now note this: "They [the nations of the world] will make war against the Lamb."

So the nations of the world join the devil on one side, while the Lamb is on the other. And who is this "Lamb"? The "Lamb" in Revelation always represents Jesus Christ.[2]

How amazing! Jesus Christ Himself will be one of the contestants in earth's final conflict! And Revelation says "the Lamb will overcome them [earth's nations] because he is Lord of lords and King of kings" (chapter 17:14).

The rider on the horse

Revelation's final picture of this battle comes in chapter 19: "I saw heaven standing open," John says, "and there before me was a white horse, whose rider is called Faithful and True. With justice he judges and makes war" (verse 11).

Revelation goes on to say that "the armies of heaven were following him, riding on white horses and dressed in fine linen, white and clean" (verse 14). The phrase "armies of heaven" probably refers to the angels (chapter 12:7-9).

We know, of course, that the devil will be on the other side. Does this passage say anyone will join him? Oh yes! John says, "I saw the beast and *the kings of the earth and their armies* gathered together to make war against the rider on the horse and his army" (chapter 19:19).

The participants in Revelation 19 are exactly the same as those in chapter 17—Jesus and His followers on one side and the devil and his followers on the other. And chapter 19 indicates the same outcome. It says "the beast was captured"— taken prisoner of war, if you please!—and was "thrown alive into the fiery lake of burning sulfur" (verse 20).

Just a moment ago, we read the question in Revelation 13:4, "Who can make war against [the beast]?" Chapter 19 answers that question: Jesus, the rider on the white horse, can make war against the beast—and defeat him!

Let's find out what else Revelation tells us about Armageddon.

When will it happen?

The battle of Armageddon will have two phases; the first phase will begin a short time before Jesus' second coming. In this phase the war will take the form of persecution against God's people all over the world. For example, Revelation says the forces of evil will decree that anyone who refuses to worship in the politically correct way will be killed (chapter 13:15). At this stage of the war, it will appear that the devil and his followers are winning. That's why the prophet John said the beast "will make war against the saints and . . . *conquer* them" (verse 7).

The second phase of the battle of Armageddon will be fought at Christ's second coming. Most Bible commentators agree that the word picture in Revelation 19 of Jesus and His armies riding out of heaven on white horses is a symbolic description of the second coming of Christ.

Where will it happen?

In the Hebrew language, the word *Armageddon* means "Mount of Megiddo." There is no Mount Megiddo in Palestine, but there is a valley of Megiddo. This has led many Christians to believe that earth's end-time conflict will take place in that valley.

However, as we have seen, this battle will take place between Christ and Satan and their followers. Since every human being will join one side or the other, we can conclude that Armageddon will not be limited to one spot on earth. The battlefield will be the globe.

Armageddon, you, and me

In essence, this war that we are talking about has actually been going on since Satan tempted Eve in Eden. It's the age-old conflict between good and evil, and *it's been going on inside of you and me all our lives.*

Every person involved in a war has to make choices, from the general who plans the overall strategy to the soldier crawling through the mud and grass, trying to decide whether to shoot the enemy or take him prisoner.

The battle between good and evil in your heart and mine also involves choices. What choice do you make, for example, when you have the opportunity to cheat on your income-tax return? What happens when you're burning-up angry at someone and you can either explode or keep quiet? What do you do when someone at work seems more attractive than your spouse? You and I are confronted with choices like these every day of the year.

The war is real right now!

Armageddon is still future. But it, too, will involve choices regarding spiritual and moral issues. If you don't remember anything else in this chapter, I hope you keep the following in mind: *Unless we choose to change, you and I will make the same spiritual and moral choices in earth's final conflict as we are making right now.*

The powerful beast that emerges from the sea in Revelation 13 appears to be invincible. During the first part of this conflict, nobody can make war against him. The saints (that's you and me) try, but the beast conquers them. In Revelation 19, however, the rider on the white horse engages this beast in battle, defeats him, and throws him into a lake of burning sulfur.

Revelation 17:14 says that the nations of the earth "will make war against the Lamb, but the Lamb will overcome them because he is Lord of lords and King of kings—and with him will be his called, chosen and faithful followers."

Let's unpack that verse, shall we? The most exciting part is that Jesus Christ is going to win the battle of Armageddon! And the next most exciting part is that you and I will be with Him!

Actually, I'd like to turn that around and say that Jesus will be "with" *you and me* during the battle of Armageddon. Isn't that what He promised two thousand years ago? He said, "Surely I am *with you* always, to the very end of the age" (Matthew 28:20). He's going to keep that promise right to the finish line!

Every now and then, I meet people who are so frightened of the end time that they weep and wail and wring their hands. But I get excited when I realize that *Jesus will be on your side and my side in the final conflict.* Armageddon can't hurt us, because our Leader is King over all the kings of the earth and Lord over all its lords!

But how about the devil, who started this war thousands of years ago in heaven when he rebelled against God? What will be his fate? Revelation says that the beast will be "thrown alive into the fiery lake of burning sulfur," and eventually the devil himself will be cast into this same lake of fire (chapters 19:20; 20:10).

Satan will be destroyed! That will be his reward for the havoc he's wreaked on this earth for thousands of years. Armageddon will truly be "the devil's payday."

Yes, the war is real—so real, in fact, that for a while, it will look like God's people are losing and Satan is winning. But during the battle of Armageddon, God's people will have Jesus on their side, and He will defeat all of their enemies, including the devil himself, who has been trying so desperately to destroy them.

And if we choose to put ourselves on Jesus' side today, we are assured that He will keep us on His side in the final, most intense battle this world has ever known.

---

1. Some people identify these ten kings with the nations of the European Common Market. However, John's description suggests a global conflict.

2. See, for example, Revelation 5:6. The lamb in chapter 13:11 refers to a false Christ.

chapter two

Taking the Mystery Out of End-Time Choices

During the summer of 1994, my son Barry, received four job offers. He had recently completed a master's degree in biology and was looking for employment in his chosen field.

As we were talking about his options, I asked, "Have you ever thought, Barry, that the choice you make about these job offers will determine the direction of your life for the next forty years?"

Barry made his choice—a wise one, which I think he will always be glad for. Yet if he's like me, a few years from now, he'll pause to ponder what direction his life would have taken had he accepted one of the other job opportunities.

Choices have consequences that we often cannot see when we're doing the choosing. "Two roads diverged in a wood," wrote poet Robert Frost, "and I—I took the one less traveled by, / and that has made all the difference."[1]

Consider these "what ifs":

- What if Jesus Christ had chosen not to go to the cross?
- What if John F. Kennedy had followed Jeanne Dixon's advice and not gone to Dallas that fateful day in 1963?
- What if Ronald Goldman had decided not to drop by Nicole Simpson's house the night of June 12, 1994?

The destiny of each human being is determined by his or her choices. World history is created by the choices people make—often the seemingly trivial choices of obscure individuals.

The most important choices you and I make are spiritual. If you think you are not a spiritual person, that only means you don't spend much time thinking about spiritual issues. You and I are spiritual beings by virtue of the fact that we are human. Whether we realize it or not, we make spiritual choices every day.

For example, how do you respond to someone who lashes out at you? What programs do you watch on TV? How do you divide your time between family and work? These are ordinary, everyday choices that you and I make all the time, usually with only a fleeting thought. But each one, along with a thousand others like them, is a spiritual choice, because each arises out of who we are in our inmost souls.

The book of Revelation talks about spiritual choices. Please consider with me two of the most important choices Revelation asks you and me to make.

Our relationship to Jesus

"I stand at the door and knock," Revelation quotes Jesus as saying. "If anyone hears my voice and opens the door, I will come in and eat with him, and he with me" (chapter 3:20).

The first choice Revelation confronts us with is the most important one: What will we do about Jesus?

When Jesus said, "I stand at the door and knock," He did not mean that He would knock on the front doors of our houses. The word *door* in this verse is a metaphor, a symbol, for the entrance to our hearts. Jesus meant that He wants to enter our hearts and minds.

If you've not thought much about spiritual issues, you may wonder what I mean by Jesus coming into your heart. That's a good question.

The science-fiction TV programs I've watched sometimes

refer to an energy called "the Force" that can influence the way people think and feel. That's something like what I'm referring to when I write about Jesus coming into our hearts—and what the Bible means when it talks about the "new birth" and being "born again." God changes us on the inside.

This inner change is profoundly spiritual. It affects our total outlook on life. In the preceding chapter, we talked about murder and crime and sin. Murder is a crime of hate. It's committed by people who have *not* experienced this inner transformation. When people let Jesus into their hearts, He changes their hatred to love, their resentment to forgiveness, their pride to humility.

People who have truly experienced this change nearly always report feeling much happier. Why? Because hatred, resentment, and pride cause an incredible amount of stress. But as soon as Jesus, the true "Force," touches us, a change begins in the deepest part of our spiritual nature. We begin to relax. The stress begins to drain away. Even in its earliest stages, this new experience can feel *so good*.

That's why the life of a truly transformed Christian is so different—and so happy. That's why Jesus said to His disciples, "I have told you this so that my joy may be in you and that your joy may be complete" (John 15:11).

This is what Jesus meant in Revelation 3:20 when He said that He's standing at our heart's door knocking to get in. He wants to transform us on the inside so that our whole outlook on life will be different—and so much happier.

Jesus said that when we allow Him into our hearts, He will eat with us. Eating together is one of most common things we humans do to deepen our relationships with each other. When Jesus offered to "come in and eat" with us, that was a symbolic way of saying that He wants to have a close relationship with us. And it's this relationship with Him that changes our hatred to love, our resentment to forgiveness, and our sadness to joy.

But notice that in this metaphor, Jesus is on the outside. He says He will come in and eat with us *if* we hear His voice and open the door. We don't have to let Him in. And He won't force His way in like a burglar. Whether or not He comes in is up to us.

Did you know that God is pro-choice? I don't mean that He approves of abortion, because I'm sure He doesn't. What I mean is that God made human beings free to choose their own spiritual destiny, and He will not interfere with that right. If we choose to let Him into our hearts, He will come in. If we refuse, He respects our choice and stays outside.

So the most basic choice you and I must make is what we will do about Jesus. This choice will affect every other choice we make the rest of our lives, and these choices, in turn, will affect not only our own lives but the history of the world.

Revelation is a book about prophecy and how *the spiritual choices people make affect the direction of history.* And this brings us to the second major choice that Revelation confronts us with.

Earth's final choices

Revelation predicts that history will reach a white-hot climax. A crisis will develop that will force every human being to make life-and-death decisions. This is especially evident in what Revelation 13 says about two "beast" powers. (The biblical books Daniel and Revelation both use animal figures to represent human political and religious institutions, much as modern editorial cartoonists use animal and other figures to represent nations—the eagle or Uncle Sam for the United States, the bear for Russia, etc.)

We know that these beast powers will be very spiritual, because both of them are deeply concerned about worship (see, for example, verses 4 and 15). But it's also obvious that both of these beasts will be evil.

Does that seem strange to you? Have you always associated being "spiritual" with being "good"? Then think again. To be spiritual means that you pay attention to the spiritual part of your nature—your emotions, your attitudes, the things you like and don't like.

We consider spiritual ideals to be qualities such as humility and love. However, the devil cultivates selfishness, hatred, and pride. These qualities are also very spiritual—and very evil.

The two evil end-time forces in Revelation 13 blaspheme God and persecute His people. (I'll have much more to say about these forces in upcoming chapters.) Revelation 13 indicates that these two beast powers will create circumstances that will force every human being into making profound spiritual choices. This is especially evident with respect to the second beast:

• He gave breath to the image of the beast and caused the whole world to worship it on pain of death (verse 15).

• He forced everyone to receive a mark of the first beast or suffer economic boycott (verses 16, 17).

Can you imagine someone threatening you with death just because you refused to worship his or her way? That seems inconceivable in America and Canada, where we take our freedom to worship as we please about as much for granted as we do air and water. Even today, however, there are places in our world where you would be threatened with death if you were to worship in the manner of your choice.

The Bible says that Revelation's beast power will cause *the whole world* to worship its way on pain of death. That has to include our own part of planet Earth, where we take freedom of worship so much for granted. If that sounds strange, remember that Jesus Himself said that before He comes, His followers will be "hated by all nations" because of Him (Matthew 24:9). "All nations" includes the two on the North American continent that have stood so firmly for freedom of religion.

The Bible makes it clear that this crisis will erupt in the world a short time before Jesus comes the second time. If His coming is near—and I believe it is—then in the near future, you and I will be confronted with the toughest choice of our lives: whether to worship God's way or Satan's way.

The early Christians faced that choice. They were dragged before Roman governors and offered the choice of casting a few flakes of incense onto the coals of a pagan altar and continuing to live or of refusing and being put to death.

What a cruel choice! What is a bit of incense, after all? Yet casting it on the altar meant denying the Christ who had changed them on the inside, and these early Christians were willing to die rather than to deny Him even by that tiny gesture.

Sitting in our easy chairs, it's hard to imagine that you and I may confront a choice someday that's just as cruel and just as clear-cut and simple. But it's true. In the final wrap-up of world history, the entire human race will be brought to just two options: Jesus or Satan, the seal of God or the mark of the beast.

And the problem is that the world will be in utter chaos when that happens. In fact, that's *why* it will happen. The Bible suggests that economic collapse, world war, and global natural disaster will devastate the world, and earth's leaders will create a powerful new world order just to provide every human being with the bare necessities of life.

This crisis will be the catalyst for a profound rejection of the secular presuppositions on which the human race has operated for the past five hundred years. Religion will emerge as the overarching solution to this global holocaust. The majority of earth's inhabitants will grasp at this religious solution the way a drowning person grasps at a rope.

Yet it will all be a great deception.

Jesus said, "False Christs and false prophets will appear and perform great signs and miracles to *deceive* even the elect—if that were possible" (Matthew 24:24). Paul predicted the antichrist will display "all kinds of counterfeit miracles, signs and wonders, and . . . every sort of evil that *deceives* those who are perishing" (2 Thessalonians 2:9, 10). And John used exactly the same terms to describe the second beast in Revelation 13: "He performed great and miraculous signs" by which he "*deceived* the inhabitants of the earth" (verses 13, 14).

Can you imagine what it will be like to stand up and say, "I will *not* bow down to this false religion" when the whole world is in chaos and has been swept into this great deception?

That's the decision Revelation says God's people must face just before Jesus returns.

The question is, What will you and I decide?

The answer is simple: We will make the same choice about Jesus then that we are making now. If you and I choose to invite Him into our hearts to transform us today, we will choose Him then. If we don't choose Him now, we won't choose Him then.

All choices have consequences. Sometimes those consequences are reversible, and sometimes they aren't. If today you bought a jacket at a store and then tomorrow decided you didn't like it, you could probably return it and get your money back.

Right now, you and I can reverse our decision about Jesus. If we decide against Him one day, we still have the opportunity of deciding for Him the next. But in earth's final crisis, our choice about Jesus will be final.

---

1. From "The Road Not Taken," quoted in John Bartlett, *Familiar Quotations*, 13th edition (Boston: Little, Brown and Company, 1955), 879.

chapter three

The Perfect Place to Live

"Homicide is as American as a Colt .45."

So said *Newsweek* in its August 15, 1994, issue. And the facts bear out the gruesome truth. The cover story, titled "Murder: A Week in the Death of America," reported that a stunning 24,500 persons were murdered in the United States during 1993!

And the largest single group of killers is men between the ages of fourteen and twenty-four, who commit more than half of all the murders in the nation. But even ten/eleven-year-olds are murderers today! *Newsweek* calls it "a horrifying trend that began in 1992 and . . . will only get worse." Yet murder is only a fraction of the crime wave that is sweeping America in the final decade of the millennium.

Actually, our whole world is reeling out of control. Rwanda and Bosnia are the most visible names at the time I'm writing this chapter (September 1994). A year ago it was the New York Trade Center and Somalia, and before that it was terrorism in the Middle East.

The Bible sums up our problem neatly in three letters: S-I-N—a word the world used to laugh at, but that actually makes sense now.

Did you know that prophecy talks about it too? Revelation, to be exact, the Bible book we're studying in this book. And

Revelation even uses our terms: *murder, sexual immorality, lying*, and *theft,* among others (Revelation 21:8; 9:22).

Sin is real life

Actually, even the people who laugh at the word *sin* don't like it in real life. Everywhere we hear talk about safe streets. Parents want playgrounds where they don't have to worry about some madman mowing down their children with his automatic rifle. Women want cities where they can feel safe walking downtown at midnight. We'd all love to live in a city so free of crime that city hall could fire the police force. What American, what Canadian, wouldn't move there in a flash!

Here's the good news: Revelation says it's coming. The "New Jerusalem" it's called, and Revelation says that "nothing impure will ever enter it, nor will anyone who does what is shameful or deceitful" (Revelation 21:27). And read this description: "[God] will wipe every tear from their eyes. There will be no more death or mourning or crying or pain, for the old order of things has passed away" (verse 4).

Talk about the ideal city! That's most people's dream town—and each of us has a guaranteed option to live there!

But those of us who'll be there must choose to solve the crime problem first, not in some criminal's heart, but in our own. For you see, deep down, each one of us is a criminal. Not the kind who would hold up a bank or kill children on a playground, to be sure. Just the little sins—reading a pornographic magazine, telling the boss a white lie, losing our temper at the kids.

Little sins?

There's really no such thing. Remember that one "little" exposure to AIDS will eventually destroy your whole body. Similarly, one "little" exposure to sin would eventually destroy the tranquility of the entire New Jerusalem. That's why Revelation says that "*nothing* impure will *ever* enter it." Only in this way can God absolutely guarantee 100 percent safe streets for everyone forever.

The question is, How can we solve the crime problem in our hearts so we can live in that city? Actually, we can't. But God can, and Revelation tells how.

Knowing we're criminals

We must begin by admitting we're criminals. And for most of us that's a tough choice, because we don't like to think of ourselves as sinners. So God has to point out the problem.

Chapters 2 and 3 of Revelation consist of letters that Jesus told John to write to seven churches in Asia Minor—a region that roughly encompasses what we today know as Turkey. The ancient cities where these churches were located were Ephesus, Smyrna, Pergamum, Thyatira, Sardis, Philadelphia, and Laodicea.

Jesus was very direct in pointing out the character flaws in these people's lives. "I have this against you . . . ," He said to the churches in Ephesus and Thyatira, and to the church in Pergamum, He said, "I have a few things against you."

If I were to talk to you like that, you'd think I was being rude. But that wasn't Jesus' purpose at all. He wanted to get these people's attention so they could correct the defects that would keep them out of His perfect city.

Let's take a quick look at what Jesus said to three of the seven churches. You'll see that His words apply just as much to you and me as they did to them. He's being just as direct with you and me as He was with them.

The church in Ephesus. Jesus said to the church in Ephesus, "You have forsaken your first love" (Revelation 2:4).

Is forsaking love a sin?

Absolutely. How can anyone have a safe city when the people in it don't know how to love each other? It's for lack of love that America's cities are filled with crime.

Unfortunately, when we're being selfish (which is what it means to be unloving), many of us think we're simply sticking up for our rights or taking what belongs to us in the first place. So Jesus confronts us: "You've lost your love."

The church in Thyatira. To the church in Thyatira, Jesus said, "I have this against you: You tolerate that woman Jezebel, who calls herself a prophetess. By her teaching she misleads my servants into sexual immorality" (Revelation 3:20).

Sexual immorality—among Christians?

Don't kid yourself! The problem is that Christians who get mixed up in sexual sin know it's wrong, so they have to figure out a way to make it seem right. It's called *denial.*

"How can it be wrong when it feels so right?" the adulterer asks, or, "Nobody understands how powerful my sexual urges are," or, "God understands that I can't overcome this sin, so He'll forgive me."

Sexual immorality isn't the only sin that we Christians excuse. There's also gluttony (overeating and food addictions), theft, cheating, alcohol addiction, and gambling, to name a few others. Yes, Christians do get mixed up in all of these sins, and we excuse ourselves for them.

That's why Jesus has to look us straight in the eye, point His finger at our defects, and tell us boldly, "*This* is your problem."

Jesus doesn't do this to keep us *out* of the New Jerusalem. He does it because He wants us *in* the New Jerusalem. But He knows we can't enter it if we refuse to face up to the sins in our lives that would turn the New Jerusalem into the next hotbed of crime. Breaking out of our denial of the sin in our lives is a tough choice, but it's a choice we *must* make if we want to live in God's perfect city.

The church in Laodicea. "You are neither cold nor hot," Jesus said to the church in Laodicea. "You say, 'I am rich; I have acquired wealth and do not need a thing.' But you do not realize that you are wretched, pitiful, poor, blind and naked" (Revelation 3:15, 17).

These people have a major spiritual problem. At the very moment they are congratulating themselves for being so good,

God is telling them that their lives are a mess. As they see it, they're fine, upstanding people, but God says, "If I were to let you live in My New Jerusalem, you'd turn it into a criminal's paradise."

Again, we're talking about *denial*. We humans are so anxious to look good that we'll say our face is clean when the mirror just told us it's dirty. That's why Jesus has to confront us. That's why He has to *tell* us what's wrong with our lives. We'd never recognize the problem if He didn't.

Repenting of our sins

Fortunately, Jesus doesn't stop with pointing out our sins. He also calls on us to acknowledge them, or as the Bible puts it, to repent of them.

Now that makes sense, doesn't it? Who of us wouldn't like to see every criminal in the land acknowledge their wrongs and repent of them? The best way to get safe streets, after all, is not to lock up criminals but to get them to repent of their crimes.

If you've ever been to an Alcoholics Anonymous meeting, you know that one of the things they stress most is honesty. They encourage alcoholics to acknowledge not only their destructive drinking but also the harm that their drinking has caused to their families and friends.

Wouldn't it be great if all the abusive people in the world and all the child molesters became honest, acknowledged their problems, and chose to change?

That's all that Jesus asks of you and me with our so-called little sins. "Remember the height from which you have fallen [and] repent," He said to the church in Ephesus. To the church in Laodicea, He said, "Be earnest, and repent" (Revelation 2:4; 3:19). And to you and me, He says, "Please be honest with Me and repent."

The promise to those who do

Jesus holds out a wonderful promise to those who choose to

get real with Him, who acknowledge the sins He points out to them. Let me give you a short sampling:

Ephesus

To him who overcomes, I will give the right to eat from the tree of life, which is in the paradise of God (Revelation 2:7).

Philadelphia

Him who overcomes I will make a pillar in the temple of my God (Revelation 3:12).

Laodicea

To him who overcomes, I will give the right to sit with me on my throne (Revelation 3:21).

Strange as some of this language may seem to you now, it all comes down to one thing: Jesus promises all who choose to become honest with Him and repent of their sins a place in His perfect, crime-free city. And the wonderful thing is that it doesn't matter how bad you and I may have been. He's willing to forgive everything we ever did wrong, just as long as we are willing to be honest about it and repent.

You may have thought that Revelation predicted *events*. It does. But far more importantly, Revelation describes a *spiritual conflict*. The point is that the spiritual forces of good and evil in human *hearts* work themselves out as good and evil *events* in human history.

Revelation points to a time when good and evil will reach a final climax in the world. The spiritual battle between good and evil results in acts of mercy and of murder on the streets of our cities today. In the same way, the forces of good and evil will produce actual recordable events in history's final crisis.

Please notice the spiritual forces that will be at work in this conflict. On the one side, Revelation says that God's people will "obey [his] commandments and remain faithful to Jesus" (chapter 14:12). On the other side, it says that those who oppose God will refuse to repent (chapter 16:9, 11).

So in those letters to the seven churches at the beginning of Revelation, Jesus is pointing out the spiritual choices you and I need to make in order to be ready for the events predicted at the end of Revelation.

In the following chapters, I'll be talking more about both the events in history's coming climax and the spiritual forces driving them. The most important thing you and I need to notice right now, though, is that we can't wait until earth's final crisis—the battle of Armageddon—to decide which side we will be on.

I'm going to assume that everyone reading this book *wants* to be on God's side during the battle of Armageddon. I don't know of anyone who literally wants to "go to hell." If there's an eternally bright future ahead, all of us want to be a part of it. All of us want citizenship in God's New Jerusalem with its safe playgrounds and streets.

But for that to happen, we must listen to the messages Jesus sends us about our lives right now. It may be tough looking for the crimes—the big sins and the little sins in our lives that would make us unfit citizens for God's crime-free city. It may be tough getting honest with God and ourselves and repenting of those sins.

Yet the choice is quite simple, isn't it? Which city do you and I want to live in? New York with all its crime and pain or God's New Jerusalem, where there will be no more crime, pain, tears, or death?

If you, like me, want to live in God's perfect, crime-free city, then we both need to pay careful attention to what God says about the crime in our lives right now.

Why don't you go back and read Jesus' messages to all seven churches? It's His introduction, His initial statement in the book of Revelation, which outlines the choices you and I must make in order to be ready for the climax of history that is described with such spectacular language at the end of Revelation.

chapter four

Pictures of Jesus in Revelation

Imagine, for a moment, that you are one of those people who isn't sure God exists. The way things are going in the world, you're not sure you *want* to believe in God. Still, it would be nice to know that Someone is in charge "up there." So on the chance that God really does exist, you begin reflecting on what He might be like.

What kind of God would you like to have?

"Well, for starters, I'd want a God who would do something about all the suffering in the world," you say. "I'd want Someone who would bring rain when the farmers need it and who'd heal all the sick people—especially those with handicaps and debilitating diseases. I'd want someone who would control the forces of nature a good bit better than what's happening now so that there'd be no more hurricanes, volcanoes, and earthquakes."

My guess is that you'd also like to have a God who understands you—who realizes that you are human. You do make mistakes, after all. You'd want someone who loves you and forgives you when you do wrong, not someone who threatens to fry you in fire and brimstone for every little sin you commit.

Many people also want a God who would see that justice is done. "Where is God when innocent people suffer?" they ask. Most of us, when we suffer at the hand of others, want vindication for ourselves as well. We see this in the Bible itself, even in Revelation, where the souls of the martyrs cry out, "How long, Sovereign Lord, holy and true, until you judge the inhabitants of the earth and avenge our blood?" (chapter 6:10).

There's something of a contradiction between our desire for a God who forgives the wrongs we commit against others and our wish for a God who punishes those who harm us. Nevertheless, most of us can understand the desire for vengeance, not only on the perpetrators of holocausts such as those brought on the world by Hitler, Stalin, and Idi Amin, but on those who cause us intense pain.

The Bible claims to tell us about God. So what does it say He is like? Specifically, what does Revelation say about God?

We find three pictures of Jesus in Revelation, and I'd like to show you that in these three pictures, we see exactly the kind of God we've just been talking about—exactly the kind of God we'd choose to run the universe if the choice could be ours.[1]

What Jesus does about our suffering

John, the author of Revelation, had been a disciple of Jesus many years before. Now he was a prisoner on the island of Patmos—a desolate speck of rock jutting out of the Mediterranean Sea off the coast of Asia Minor (what is now Turkey). In the eyes of the Roman courts, John had committed the "crime" of being a follower of Jesus. He was being persecuted for his faith.

Patmos is not an ideal place to live. I'm sure the wind blows cold across the island, especially in the winter. Even as an old man (he was probably around ninety years old at the time), John may have been forced into hard labor. He must have suffered a lot on Patmos.

It's in this setting that Revelation gives us our first picture of Jesus. We find it in chapter 1, and it shows us how God relates to human suffering.

John doesn't tell us where on the island of Patmos he was at the time of this vision, but in my mind I see him sitting on a cliff overlooking the sea. Perhaps he's praying, asking God to deliver him. What good, after all, can he accomplish on this barren island?

Suddenly, John hears a voice behind him (verse 10), and he turns around to see who has interrupted his meditation. To his surprise, he sees his old friend Jesus—the very One he had walked and talked with years before back in Palestine! Jesus is dressed like an Old Testament high priest, although the way He is dressed isn't really important to our discussion.

What matters is that Jesus is there.

Most of us, when we fall on hard times, want a God who will get us out of trouble. Sometimes God does deliver believers. But God hasn't promised to get us out of all our troubles in this life. To the contrary, Jesus warned His disciples that "in this world you will have trouble" (John 16:33).

If God doesn't deliver us from all our troubles, what does He do for us? That's where the story of John on the island of Patmos comes in. When John found himself in trouble on that desolate, wind-blown piece of rock, Jesus was there with him.

Anytime God chooses not to deliver us from trouble, He joins us in it!

Come on, you say. Revelation is about kingdoms and global wars and beast powers that chew up the world. It has much more important things to talk about than God joining people when they're in trouble.

It's true that Revelation talks about world powers, especially those at the end of time. But if you read Revelation carefully, you will discover that it's about those world powers attacking God's people. The first beast power in Revelation 13 makes war with the saints (verse 7), while the second beast power threatens with death anyone who does not worship in the politically correct manner (verse 15). And in chapter 17, the woman called Babylon is drunk with the blood of the saints (verse 6).

Yes, Revelation is about beast powers, all right. It describes the fearsome attacks these powers will make on God's people at the very end of time. And suddenly it becomes very important whether Jesus is *with* His people when they're in trouble!

While God does sometimes deliver His people from trouble, Revelation does not promise that He always will. Jesus did not deliver John from his suffering on Patmos. He joined him in his troubles. David said that whenever he walked through the valley of the shadow of death, God was *with* him (see Psalm 23:4), and Jesus promised to be *with us* always, to the end of the age (see Matthew 28:20).

In fact, the very reason Jesus came to this earth two thousand years ago and lived more than thirty years among us was so that He could be *with us* in our troubles. His name *Immanuel* is a Hebrew word that means "God with us" (Matthew 1:28)!

Jesus suffered the same poverty that many of us must bear, and He even experienced the death that will come to each of us someday. Not only that, the manner of His death was far worse than most of us will ever have to endure. Thus, even in His death on the cross, Jesus was *with* the people He cared about.

And this brings us to the next picture of Jesus in Revelation. We find it in chapter 5.

What Jesus does about our sins

The picture of Jesus in chapter 1 was quite literal. We saw Jesus about the way He probably looks. But in Revelation 5, the picture is highly symbolic—so symbolic, in fact, that it makes you wonder what about it could possibly be real. Let's begin with a bit of background.

Revelation 4 shows us God seated on His throne, and in verse 1 of chapter 5, we see Him holding a scroll in His right hand. We are not told what's written on the scroll, but it must be important, because John actually wept when no one could be found worthy to open the scroll (verses 3, 4).

Fortunately, one Person was found worthy to open the scroll: Jesus. Revelation doesn't call Him "Jesus," though. It says "the

Lion of the tribe of Judah, the Root of David, has triumphed. He is able to open the scroll" (verse 5). ("Lion of the tribe of Judah" and "Root of David" are biblical metaphors that refer to Jesus.)

At this point in the story, John the Revelator does something very interesting. Without so much as a word of explanation, he switches symbols on us. And what a switch it is! In the very next verse after calling Jesus "the Lion of the tribe of Judah," he says "then I saw a Lamb."

That's Jesus again, and the metaphors are quite a contrast— from a lion to a lamb! At the very least, the switch should make for some interesting discussion. But John's reason for giving us these diametrically opposite images of Jesus is not our concern here. Our purpose is to understand how God relates to people who make mistakes—who sin. And to understand that, we have to read just a bit more about Jesus as the Lamb.

"Then I saw a Lamb, looking as if it had been slain," John said, and he added that the Lamb "was standing in the center of the throne" (verse 6).

The focus here is Jesus' death on the cross, which has everything to do with the sins and moral mistakes you and I so often make. For you see, His death on the cross opened the way for our sins to be forgiven. Before He was even born, the angel Gabriel announced that the most important reason why Jesus came to this world was to "save his people from their sins" (Matthew 1:21). That's the very kind of God that most people—when they think their most ideal thoughts about Him—are looking for. (May I suggest that the picture of God as a tyrant who can't wait to punish people for their sins has turned more people away from the Christian faith than has just about anything else?)

Jesus Himself demonstrated this forgiveness on the cross when He prayed for those crucifying Him, "Father, forgive them, for they do not know what they are doing" (Luke 23:34).

This brings us to the final picture of Jesus in Revelation.

What Jesus does about injustice

In Revelation 19:11, we see Jesus dressed in white, riding a white horse out of heaven. An army of beings dressed in white follows Him, and they are also riding white horses (verse 14). As we continue reading in chapter 19, we discover that Jesus is riding out of heaven to do battle with the kings of the earth and their armies (verse 19).

This description actually pictures earth's final battle—what Revelation calls the battle of Armageddon (see chapter 11 of this book). However, I want you to notice the purpose of this war. Speaking of Jesus, the Rider on the horse, verse 11 says, "With justice he judges and makes war."

There we have it: The purpose of this war is to bring justice into the earth. Someday, all of the Neros, all of the Hitlers, all of the Idi Amins, and every other tyrant who has inflicted suffering on innocent human beings will be called to account.[2]

Two thousand years ago, Jesus Himself said that the day is coming when everyone will be rewarded according to his or her deeds (Revelation 22:12; John 5:28, 29). The 19th and 20th chapters of Revelation show us when that will be. At that time, the prayer of the martyrs, "How long, Sovereign Lord, until You judge the inhabitants of the earth and avenge our blood?" will be answered.

If you have suffered injustice at the hands of people with evil motives, those people will be called to account someday. This does not mean that God is unwilling to forgive them. But forgiveness requires repentance, and if your persecutors do not repent before the time for repentance has passed,[3] they must account for their evil deeds.

And this brings us full circle, back to the first item that we discussed in this chapter—the desire each of us has deep down for a God who will *do something* about the suffering in the world. So much of that suffering is inflicted unjustly on innocent people. Maybe you yourself have suffered an injustice. Perhaps right now you are in pain from an injustice.

The world you and I live in is an unjust world. Nobody ever promised that this present life would be fair. Certainly God has not made that kind of promise. Nor has Jesus.

But God has promised that if we repent and confess the injustices we commit against others, He will forgive us. And He has promised that a day is coming when He will avenge the injustices done to us and all other innocent people in the world. "Vengeance is mine," He once said. "I will repay" (Romans 12:19, KJV).

Many people think Revelation describes a horrible God who can't wait to bring fire and brimstone down on His enemies. The fire and brimstone are there, to be sure. But Revelation's most important message is that God cares so much about His people that He joins them in their suffering. He forgives those who are sorry for their sins and turn from them.

And whether we suffer the fire and brimstone with which God will cleanse the universe of sin and suffering or whether we enjoy God's forgiveness and vindication depends entirely on us—on whether we *choose* to place ourselves on God's side now.

I hope that you can now see in Revelation a God, a Jesus, whom you'll *want* to choose as your best Friend! Because when you make that choice, you are assured of a place in His eternal kingdom.

---

1. Most Christians, because they accept Jesus as God in the fullest sense, would agree that what Jesus does in Revelation is God in action. Even if you happen not to agree, I'm sure you'd be willing to admit that in these three scenes, Jesus is acting on behalf of God, so that what He does is what God would do.

2. At the second coming of Christ, which Revelation 19 describes, the only ones called to account will be those who are alive on the earth at that time. Those tyrants who died earlier in earth's history will be called to account at the end of the millennium (see Revelation 20:11, 12).

3. See chapter 8 of this book.

chapter five

The Deadly End-Time Masquerade

Susan Smith.

You remember her, don't you—the woman in Union, South Carolina, who murdered her children in October 1994? She claimed that a black man stole her car at gunpoint and took her two boys, Michael and Alexander, ages three and one, along with the car.

Hundreds of people in Union searched the roads and woods around the town for the boys. And Susan and her estranged husband, David, appeared on national TV, pleading for the return of their children.

Everyone believed Susan's story. "There's no way . . . [she] had anything to do with what happened to those children," declared a next-door neighbor.

Then Susan confessed. She had killed the children herself—strapped them in her car, then watched as it rolled into a lake and sank.

Instantly, the horrified town turned against Susan with loathing. The townspeople felt betrayed and angry. They sneered and hissed and called her unprintable names. Given the chance, some of them would have inflicted their own version of capital punishment on her.

End-time impostors

Strange as it may seem, this tragic story has striking similarities to events portrayed in Revelation. Before getting into that, though, let's check out a bit of background. We need to examine three predictions Jesus made about the end time.

Deception. Jesus warned that just before His second coming, many false Christs and false prophets would arise, deceiving many people, and that one of their favorite ways of deceiving would be the miracles they perform. So clever will these impostors be, Jesus said, that Christians themselves will be in danger of falling for their deceptions (see Matthew 24:24).

There's a fairly widespread belief among Christians today that the end-time antichrist will be an evil person who rules the world with an iron fist. But such a person wouldn't deceive anyone. To deceive, a false Christ must look and act so much like the real Christ that even Christians believe it's really Him.

Self-deception. Jesus also said that many end-time Christians would be self-deceived. He predicted that at His second coming, many will say to Him, " 'Lord, Lord, did we not prophesy in your name, and in your name drive out demons and perform many miracles?' Then I [Jesus] will tell them plainly, 'I never knew you. Away from me, you evildoers!' " (Matthew 7:22, 23).

Notice that these people know exactly who Jesus is. They claim to be loyal servants and are shocked to learn that He absolutely rejects them. They are the victims of a horrible delusion. All along, they've thought they were saved, only to discover at the very end that they are lost. These are the very people who will fall for the deceptions of the antichrist.

Betrayal. Jesus also predicted that at the end of time, some Christians will turn against other Christians. Can you imagine that? Actually, it happened to Jesus Himself. Judas, one of His own disciples, betrayed Him, and within twenty-four hours, Jesus was hanging on a cross.

Jesus said you and I will be betrayed just like He was. "A

time is coming," He said, "when anyone who kills you will think he is offering a service to God" (John 16:2). The name for that is persecution. Christians will be persecuting Christians during the weeks and months that lead up to Christ's second coming.

To summarize, Jesus predicted that the end-time antichrist will look so much like the real Christ that many Christians will be deceived into making terribly wrong choices. In their delusion, they will betray their fellow Christians, all the while thinking they are serving God.

If Jesus predicted false Christs, deception, and betrayal, then we need not be surprised to read about these same issues in Revelation. In fact, if we take Jesus' words seriously, we should *expect* to find these issues in Revelation!

Let's look at the evidence.

False Christianity in Revelation 13

We will begin with Revelation 13, where two beast powers enter the stage of the world—one from the sea and the other from the earth.

The sea beast (Revelation 13:1-10). The first beast looks horrible. It has seven heads and ten horns, a body like a leopard, the feet of a bear, and the mouth of a lion. Most significant is the fact that it gets its authority from a dragon, which in Revelation is a symbol of Satan (chapter 12:9). Clearly, this is one of the "bad guys."

Fortunately, one of the beast's heads gets a fatal wound.

Unfortunately, the fatal wound is healed.

And, amazingly, Revelation predicts that all the people in the world—five billion, by today's count—are astonished at the healing of the fatal wound, and *they worship the beast!*

Please notice two important points. First, worship is a religious act. So whatever earthly end-time power this beast represents, it will be religious.

And second, worship is a choice. We worship whatever or

whomever we *choose* to worship. And these people whom Revelation describes *choose* to worship this evil beast power.

Verse 7 indicates that this beast will be a persecuting power. It says, "He [the sea beast] was given power to make war against the saints and to conquer them."

This verse tells us one more thing about this sea beast: It has worldwide political power. The second half of the verse says, "He was given authority over every tribe, people, language, and nation."

Suddenly, everything Jesus said about false Christs and deluded Christians thinking they are doing God a service when they kill other Christians starts falling together, right here in Revelation.

Some might argue that, Yes, this beast is religious, but that doesn't necessarily mean it is Christian. It could be Muslim or Hindu or even New Age.

Good point! Keep reading.

The land beast (Revelation 13:11-18). In the very first verse of this passage, we discover the evidence that the land beast is a Christian power. "Then I saw another beast," Revelation says. "He had two horns like a lamb, but he spoke like a dragon" (verse 11).

In Revelation, a lamb always represents Jesus Christ—except here. In this one case, the "lamb" represents the false Christs that Jesus predicted would arise in the world at the end of time.

How do we know?

The best evidence that the lamb spoken of here is a *false* Christ is that (1) it looks like Jesus the Lamb, but it speaks like Satan the dragon, and (2) it performs miracles to deceive people—just like the false Christs that Jesus foretold.

Notice, also, what this land beast does: It orders the inhabitants of the world to set up an image to the sea beast (verse 14), and then it forces everyone to worship the image, threatening with capital punishment those who refuse to worship (verse 15).

All this brings us straight back to Jesus' prediction that a time is coming when "anyone who kills you will think he is offering a service to God" (John 16:2; see also Matthew 10:21).

Thus the land beast is clearly a false Christian power. And the fact that it sets up an image to the sea beast and forces the world to worship the image suggests that the first beast, if not actually Christian, is sympathetic to the false Christianity of its time.

False Christianity in Revelation 17

One other place in Revelation describes this same condition at the end of time, just before Jesus comes. That's chapter 17.

In chapter 17, an angel shows John a horrible scarlet beast with a woman riding on top of it. The woman's name is Babylon, and Babylon represents rebellion against God.

The Bible also points out that this woman is "drunk with the blood of the saints" (verse 6). That means she has killed them.

Clearly, Revelation 17 reveals a persecuting power that is in rebellion against God. But how do we know it's a Christian power? Because the key figure is a woman, and in Bible prophecy, a woman represents a church. The virtuous woman in chapter 12:1-6 represents God's true church, while the harlot in chapter 17 represents the church in deep apostasy.

Chapter 17's harlot parallels the sea beast of chapter 13 in another important way. You will recall that the sea beast had worldwide political power. So does the woman of Revelation 17.

We know this because in Bible prophecy a beast nearly always represents a major political power. Revelation 17:12 says that the ten horns on the beast are ten kings, which probably means the collective nations of the world at the very end of time. And these horns will "give their power and authority to the beast" (verse 13). In other words, this beast will receive worldwide political authority.

While it is true that the beast, which represents the state, is the one that receives worldwide authority, the clear implication is that the woman, who represents the church, wields that authority. This is obvious from the fact that the woman is riding the beast, and whether it is a horse, a donkey, a camel, or an elephant, riders control the beasts that they ride.

Revelation is actually predicting that just before Jesus returns to this earth, a worldwide union between church and state that God disapproves of will exist!

Once more, Revelation is a summary—or perhaps we should say, an expansion—of what Jesus predicted about false Christs who deceive and about Christians who kill other Christians, thinking that God will be pleased.

The fall of the antichrist

But the most significant part is yet to come. Revelation 17:16 says that "the beast and the ten horns you saw will hate the prostitute. They will bring her to ruin and leave her naked; they will eat her flesh and burn her with fire."

Why will the nations of the world destroy, in such a brutal way, the woman riding the beast? For the answer to that question, let's go back to the story of Susan Smith and examine carefully what happened.

At first, the people in her hometown believed her story and staunchly defended her. Even when the local authorities suggested she might not be telling the truth, her friends and neighbors said "No way!"

But when the truth came out, they felt betrayed. And the fierce loyalty they had felt one moment was transformed the next into an antagonism that was just as strong, if not stronger.

People whose trust has been betrayed feel profoundly bitter.

In some way that the Bible does not reveal, the true nature of the false Christian power that rules the world at the end of time will be exposed just before Jesus comes back. The harlot's mask will be stripped away, and the world will see her for what she really is—a deceiver. And they will turn on her with loathing. Their bitterness and anger will be even stronger than the loyalty they felt when she had their support.

The key question

While the Bible does not name names, I believe it gives us an accurate picture of the political and spiritual dynamics that will exist in the world shortly before Jesus returns. If I'm correct in my conviction that the coming of Jesus is near, then these political and spiritual powers are already developing and will soon be unleashed in their full force.

So here are the questions that come to you and me in this critical hour of earth's history: How can we avoid being deceived? How can we be sure that we maintain our stand firmly on the side of right in earth's darkest hour?

I will suggest three ways we can avoid deception and stand firm. *First, we must choose to stay close to Jesus.* We cannot recognize the deceptive end-time powers on our own. To understand, we must have the power of God's Spirit working within us.

And how can we access that power?

Jesus once said to His disciples, "I am the vine; you are the branches. If a man remains in me and I in him, he will bear much fruit; apart from me you can do nothing" (John 15:5). To remain in Jesus means to learn about Him each day through His Word. Make it a point to study your Bible and to pray at least once each day. My favorite time for communicating with Him in this way is early in the morning, before breakfast.

When Jesus remains in our hearts, He gives us a new outlook on life. We understand right and wrong in a totally new way. God's way of life, which used to seem so absurd, now makes perfectly good sense.

When people first become Christians, they often say that things they used to think unimportant now suddenly become very important, and things they used to think were quite all right they now realize are wrong. And not only do they consider them wrong; their new life in Jesus makes those things undesirable!

A close, personal relationship with Jesus that transforms your way of thinking and feeling is the very best—indeed, it is the only—guarantee that you will not be deceived by the false Christs and the antichrists in the end time.

Second, we must choose to learn all we can about the end time. The information I shared with you in this chapter, that Revelation's evil end-time powers are religious and professedly Christian, will help you to be cautious about accepting everything that comes along claiming to speak for God. The entire Bible is filled with information that will help you to maintain your stand firmly on God's side during the impending conflict.

Third, we must choose—indeed, we must determine—to obey God. The Bible says that God's end-time people will be a commandment-keeping people (see Revelation 12:17; 14:12). This doesn't mean that they are trying to work their way to heaven or that they think they can get God's approval through their good works. But it does mean that God's people are always committed to following wherever He leads, which is simply another way of saying that they obey Him.

Jesus once said, "If anyone chooses to do God's will, he will find out whether my teaching comes from God or whether I speak on my own" (John 7:17). If you choose to obey God regardless of how painful it may be to your natural self, you will not be deceived when the terrible forces of evil are unleashed on the world in earth's final conflict.

chapter six

Angels on a Mission

Some time ago I heard the story of a young man who grew up believing that it was his Christian duty to "witness." He felt very uncomfortable talking to people about his religion, but he often did it anyway—because he was "supposed to." The conflict between his discomfort at witnessing and the guilt he felt when he didn't witness kept getting worse and worse. Finally, unable to endure the emotional pain any longer, he went to see his pastor.

The minister listened as the young man explained the problem. When he was through, the pastor leaned back in his chair, thought a minute, and then said, "God does not require you to witness."

The young man was stunned, but after fifteen or twenty minutes of conversation with the pastor, he finally became convinced. God really did not require him to witness. What a relief! For the first time in his life, he felt good about being a Christian!

As he was leaving the church, the young man met a friend just coming up the front steps. Grabbing his friend by the arm, he all but shouted in his ear, "I've just learned the most wonderful news about God! He doesn't require me to witness!"

Reflect a bit on that story with me, would you? When we share news out of a sense of duty, the message always comes off wrong. The most successful sharing (*witnessing*, if you please) happens when we're excited about some good news—such as when parents announce the birth of their baby. This kind of witnessing is effortless. We do it without even thinking. Furthermore, everyone else enjoys hearing it.

The wise pastor understood this. He knew that the young man's "witnessing" would do him and others more harm than good as long as he thought he *had* to do it. By relieving the young man of this burden, he gave him a reason to be excited about God. He freed him to really witness about God's love—which he did the moment he left the church!

I think that's why, when Jesus told His disciples that He wanted them to be witnesses for Him, He said, "Wait until the Holy Spirit comes on you" (see Acts 1:8). Witnessing for God is never so important that we have to do it whether we feel like it or not.

When God's Spirit finally did fill Jesus' disciples, Peter preached such a powerful sermon that three thousand people became Christians in one day. That's what enthusiastic witnessing can do!

Three angels in the sky

Revelation tells us that this same kind of powerful witnessing will happen again, shortly before Jesus comes—and for the same reason: There'll be an urgency about the message that compels God's people to proclaim it. You can read about it in Revelation 14:6-12, and there's an "additional note" in chapter 18:1-4.

In chapter 14 John tells of three angels he saw flying across the sky with a message for humans. Does this mean that any day now we can expect to see three angels in the sky proclaiming God's will to the human race? Of course not. Jesus didn't commission angels to spread the good news about His life and death to all the world. He gave that responsibility to His followers—you and me. Revelation is a symbolic book. These three angels are a symbolic way of representing the witnessing of God's people at the very end of time.

God's people will proclaim the messages of these three angels all over the world—or, as Revelation puts it, "to every nation, tribe, language and people."[1] Whatever these messages are, you can expect to hear them on your TV one of these days. And I'll guarantee you one other thing: They will grab your attention, because the people proclaiming them will be excited about them.

How do I know?

Because it wouldn't be fair of God to let anyone miss hearing them. Keep reading, and you'll see why.

The first angel's message

Do me a favor. Next time you turn on your TV, notice how many of the ads offer security and peace of mind. That says something about us humans. We are constantly searching for happiness.

That's just what the first angel offers. Revelation says the first angel proclaims "the eternal gospel." The word *gospel* means the good news that Jesus died so you and I can live eternally with Him. It means the good news that God offers a way out of our dysfunctional modes of thinking and doing. With God's help *we can change.* We can be happy. We can feel fulfilled. We can have hope.

No wonder Revelation says this message is to go "to every nation, tribe, language and people." God is offering people everywhere the chance to be happier, more mature individuals. God's people can't help but get excited about preaching this message!

It's an end-time message too. The angel "said in a loud voice, 'Fear God and give him glory, because *the hour of his judgment has come.*' " God's final judgment will already be in progress when His people proclaim their message.

God's judgment-hour message is more than just *good* news

to make us feel good, though. It's also *serious* news. If you've ever sat in a courtroom during a trial, you know that it's not the place to go if you're looking for laughs. Tough decisions are made there, and sometimes people cry. The good news about God's judgment, of course, is that He's always fair.

The first angel concludes his message to the world with these words: "Worship him who made the heavens, the earth, the sea and the springs of water." In other words, God wants His people in the end time to worship Him as the Creator. That certainly is a relevant message in a day when almost the entire world attributes the origin of all life and even of the universe itself to the random forces of nature rather than to God.

The second angel's message

The second angel's message is short—just eighteen words—and it, too, is serious. Very serious. "Fallen! Fallen is Babylon the Great, which made all the nations drink the maddening wine of her adulteries."

Perhaps the second angel's message is short because it's repeated in chapter 18:1-4 with a lot more information about why Babylon has fallen. Let's read those verses, and then we'll talk about both messages:

> After this I saw another angel coming down from heaven. He had great authority, and the earth was illuminated by his splendor. With a mighty voice he shouted:
> "Fallen! Fallen is Babylon the Great!
> She has become a home for demons
> and a haunt for every evil spirit,
> a haunt for every unclean and detestable bird.
> For all the nations have drunk the maddening wine of her adulteries.
> The kings of the earth committed adultery with her,
> and the merchants of the earth grew rich from her excessive luxuries."

Then I heard another voice from heaven say:
"Come out of her, my people,
so that you will not share in her sins,
so that you will not receive any of her plagues."

From these verses you can begin to see why I said that you'll recognize the preaching of God's people when you see it on your TV. For starters, notice that Revelation goes out of its way to mention that this angel has great authority. As we already learned from Revelation 14, an angel flying in the sky with a message for the world really represents God's people preaching to the world. *It's God's people who will preach with this powerful authority.* That'll grab the attention of anyone watching TV!

The angel in Revelation 18 begins by quoting the message of the second angel in chapter 14—"Fallen! Fallen is Babylon the Great!"

Next, the angel of Revelation 18 explains what he and the angel from Revelation 14 mean when they say that Babylon has fallen. Babylon, as you may recall from the preceding chapter, symbolizes the false religion that will exist in the world at the very end of time. The angel of Revelation 18 explains that Babylon "has become a home for demons and a haunt for every evil spirit, a haunt for every unclean and detestable bird."

That's like reading a page out of today's news magazines! Why can I say this so positively?

We live in an age of profound spiritual change. For more than 1,500 years, the dominant religion of the West has been Christianity. However, beginning in the 1960s and increasingly on into the present, North Americans in particular have been experimenting with all kinds of spiritual options, including New Age theologies, Oriental mysticism, the occult, and Native American religions. America today is a smorgasbord of religious options, with everyone being his or her own authority on what constitutes authentic religion. This has created an exceptional amount of religious confusion.

And, unfortunately, this confusion is affecting Christianity itself, both Catholic and Protestant. For example, in the fall of 1993, some two thousand Protestant and Catholic women met in Minneapolis, where, among other things, they worshiped a goddess whom they called Sophia. The second angel of Revelation 14 is warning God's people to beware of this religious confusion.

God's people will also warn the world about a union of the church with the state. Revelation says that "the kings of the earth committed adultery with her [Babylon]."

When Satan came to Jesus in the wilderness, one of his temptations was to show Him "all the kingdoms of the world and their splendor. All this I will give you," Satan said, "if you will bow down and worship me" (Matthew 4:8, 9). According to Revelation, at the end of time a major portion of the world's Christian population will unite with the state, accepting the temptation that Jesus rejected.

No wonder God calls on His followers to warn the world about false end-time religion! It should hardly come as a surprise that He says to His people all over the world, "Come out of this religious smorgasbord that includes even the occult. Separate from any religion that unites with the state to compel the conscience."

The third angel's message

If the messages of the first two angels didn't get your attention, that of the third will. This angel warns the world not to worship the sea beast of Revelation 13 or receive its mark. Whoever does receive the mark, the angel says, "will drink of the wine of God's fury, which has been poured full strength into the cup of his wrath" (Revelation 14:10).

We'll be talking more about this mark of the sea beast in chapter 8 of this book. For now, though, it's enough to know that receiving the mark means accepting the false forms of religion that will exist in the world at the end of time.

Does it surprise you that the whole world—including many professed Christians—will be swept into a false religion shortly before Jesus comes? It shouldn't. Jesus Himself warned that one of the signs of His return would be false Christs and false prophets who would "deceive even the elect—if that were possible" (Matthew 24:24).

That's why you and I need to be so careful about the choices we make from the spiritual smorgasbord that is filling the world at the present time! We especially need to be careful what we mix in with our Christianity.

A spiritual conflict

A terrible spiritual conflict will grip the world in the final hours of earth's history. God's people will be on one side, and the forces of evil will be on the other. Nothing is more clear from Revelation than that.

One of the primary responsibilities of God's people at that time will be to clarify for the world the truth about God, His love, His law, and His plan to save human beings from sin. Satan and his human agents will oppose these truths bitterly. At the very least, this must surely mean that God's people will face incredible opposition to their preaching. However, God's Spirit will so fill their hearts that they will be completely possessed by His message. All the legions of hell will not be able to silence their enthusiasm. This will be witnessing at its absolute best!

You really won't be able to miss the messages of the angels of Revelation 14 and 18 when you see them on your TV. Do me a favor, will you? Pray that God will help you not only to recognize these messages but to accept them.

Better yet, why not ask God to let you have a part in proclaiming them?

---

1. Revelation mentions a worldwide proclamation only in connection with the first message, but the context makes it clear that all three of them will be proclaimed all over the earth.

Conquering Life's Highest Mountains

"Night on the South Col. The wind screeches across the ridge and sets the canvas cracking like a rifle range; an awful noise. I'm braced between Tenzing and the tent wall, no room to stretch out. Whenever my head falls back against the roof it's as if I'd run my brain into a pneumatic drill.

"The other side of Tenzing are Alf Gregory and George Lowe, hunched up in their sleeping bags, twisting, heaving around, trying to find some position less cold and miserable. . . .

"I keep looking at my watch, wondering if it's stopped. The hour hand finally creeps around to 4, and I strike a match. The thermometer on the tent wall reads: -13° F. It is still pitch dark."[1]

Who in the world? What in the world? Were these people forced to land at the North Pole when their plane ran out of gas?

Why they endured

Nothing that complicated, actually. They *chose* to sleep that way.

Who would ever choose to endure such misery—and why?

The "why" is quite simple: Mt. Everest. For what you just read are the opening lines of Sir Edmund Hillary's *National Geographic* account of his journey to the summit of earth's highest mountain. On May 29, 1953, Hillary, a New Zealander, and his Nepalese climbing companion, Tenzing Norgay, became the first humans to conquer Mt. Everest.

Hillary and Norgay *chose* to climb Mt. Everest. But they not only chose to, they were *driven* to climb it—not by any dictator or slave driver, but by the mountain's sheer presence and the fact that it had never been conquered.

Revelation talks about people like that. People who are driven for God and Jesus Christ. People who conquer mountains of the spirit—mountains of sin and slavery to human passion.

Yes, Revelation talks about people like that: "I looked, and there before me was the Lamb, standing on Mount Zion, and with him 144,000 who had his name and his Father's name written on their foreheads" (Revelation 14:1).

In one sense, the climb up Mount Zion is easy. Jesus did it for us. All He asks us to do is to confess the wrong things in our lives and accept His payment for them on the cross. Forgiveness is instantaneous, and so is salvation.

If you've ever wondered, and perhaps worried, whether you'll spend eternity in God's kingdom, you can relax. If you've already accepted Jesus as your Saviour, then you are assured of a place in God's kingdom. And if you haven't, that assurance is only a prayer away.

However, those who accept Jesus as their Saviour are immediately confronted with a challenge far greater than anything Hillary and Norgay endured on their way to the summit of Mt. Everest. For God calls upon His people to conquer the defects in their characters that dishonor Him and bring pain to others. The Bible says that the 144,000[2] we read about a moment ago will have this victorious character. Let's find out what else Revelation says about them.

Name on their foreheads

Chapter 7:4 says that the 144,000 will have the seal of God placed on their foreheads, and chapter 14:1 says they will have God's name written on their foreheads. These texts don't mean that we should start looking for the word *God* stamped on people's foreheads. The forehead symbolizes the mind. Revelation is telling us that the 144,000 will be absolutely committed to God and His way of life.

Revelation 12:17 and 14:12 suggest this same idea:[3]

The dragon was enraged at the woman and went off to make war against the rest of her offspring—those who obey God's commandments and hold to the testimony of Jesus (Revelation 12:17).

This calls for patient endurance on the part of the saints who obey God's commandments and remain faithful to Jesus (Revelation 14:12).

Notice that both these verses tell us that God's end-time people will keep His commandments. On one occasion, Jesus said to His disciples, "If you love me, you will obey what I command" (John 14:15). Obedience is a mark of loyalty, of commitment to the one obeyed. It's possible to obey someone out of fear—at the point of a gun, say, or the lash of a whip. But love is the only basis for a commitment to God and Jesus Christ. God's end-time people will choose to obey Him because they love Him.

I'm sure Jesus had the Ten Commandments in mind when He asked His disciples to obey Him, and I'm sure that in Revelation, John had the Ten Commandments in mind when he said God's end-time people will keep the commandments. But we must remember that the Ten Commandments are only a brief summary of God's will. The rest of the Bible elaborates on the principles found in the Ten Commandments. Revelation is telling us that God's end-time people will be totally committed to following Jesus wherever He leads them. Chapter 14:4 says "they follow the Lamb [Jesus] wherever he goes."

There's a saying—someone told me it originated with the Baptists—that goes like this: "God said it; I believe it; that settles it."

I like that. It's the language of total commitment. It summarizes the commitment of God's people to Jesus. That's why Revelation says they will "obey God's commandments" and "follow the Lamb wherever he goes."

Revelation goes on to say of the 144,000 that "they are blameless" (verse 5). In other words, they are perfect.

Now, theologians have debated the meaning of Christian perfection for two thousand years, so it's not likely that we'll settle the issue in this short chapter. But in just seven brief words that precede its statement of the perfection of these people, Revelation points out what I believe is the most important quality of perfect people. It says, "No lie was found in their mouths" (verse 5).

In other words, it's honesty that characterizes perfect people.

The greatest challenge

Honesty is the greatest challenge that Christianity holds out to the human race. Jesus, the founder of the Christian faith, summarized it in just two verses. In the first one, He defined dishonesty, and in the next one, He defined honesty. Let's examine them one at a time.

"Everyone who does evil hates the light," Jesus said, "and will not come into the light for fear that his deeds will be exposed" (John 3:20). "Light" in the sense in which Jesus used it here is a metaphor, or symbol, for truth. To hate the light, to hate the truth, means that we refuse to face up to what we are really like. That's dishonesty.

Jesus went on to define honesty: "Whoever lives by the truth comes into the light," He said, "so that it may be seen plainly that what he has done has been done through God" (verse 21).

Honest people may tremble at the truth, but they love it. And they don't wait for it to show up on their doorstep, either. They go after it, because in spite of the pain it causes, in the end, the truth is very liberating. That's what Jesus meant when He said, "You will know the truth, and the truth will set you free" (John 8:32).

An important aspect of both dishonesty and honesty is choice. In his book *People of the Lie*, M. Scott Peck points out that we humans "become evil over time through a long series of choices."[4] That's essentially what Jesus meant when He said that evil people "will not come into the light for fear that [their] deeds will be exposed." They *choose* not to learn the truth about their warped and twisted lives.

The irony is that evil people reject the truth about themselves *because they want to look good!* What they really want is their own selfish way, but they want to get it in a way that will make others think them unselfish.

The selfishness of evil people always inflicts pain on those around them. They do not intend to inflict pain. Most would deny that they inflict pain. But they do. That's why evil is evil. It hurts others.

Most of us have no difficulty recognizing that Adolf Hitler, Joseph Stalin, and Idi Amin were evil people. We often fail, however, to understand that evil people live among us all the time. They are our neighbors, our family members. In fact, they are us! For there is something of evil, something that causes pain to others, in each of us.

Yet the essence of evil people is not that they do evil things. It is, rather, that they refuse to acknowledge their wrongdoing. Jesus said that evil people hate the light and will not come into the light for fear that their deeds will be exposed. Paul said exactly the same thing about evil people in the end time: They perish because they chose not to love the truth and so be saved (see 2 Thessalonians 2:10).

Contrast this, now, with the honesty of God's people in the end time. Revelation says, "No lie was found in their mouths." And it adds, "They are blameless." Their blamelessness, their perfection, if you please, lies in their honesty—in their willingness to acknowledge their faults and in their desire to learn more about their inner sickness so that they can be healed. And that also is a choice.

Mental and spiritual health

M. Scott Peck defined mental health as "an ongoing process of dedication to reality at all costs."[5] That's the "coming into the light" that Jesus spoke about. For only reality—the truth about one's self—can lead to genuine spiritual health and happiness. And only those who choose that reality "at all costs" will achieve this genuine health.

The problem for us humans is that reality—the truth—has a bite to it. It chews at our pride and tears it open, exposing it the way a lion tears open a carcass and lays its innards bare. And the innards of our souls are not pleasant to look at. It's much easier to put on a front, fooling ourselves all the time and others some of the time (but God none of the time) into thinking that we are really quite good. Admitting our wrongdoing to ourselves, and especially to other people, is profoundly painful. Coming into the light so that our deeds can be exposed is one of the most painful choices a human being can make.

Paul expressed that pain when he said:

I do not understand what I do. For what I want to do I do not do, but what I hate I do. . . .

For in my inner being I delight in God's law; but I see another law at work in the members of my body, waging war against the law of my mind and making me a prisoner of the law of sin at work within my members. What a wretched man I am! Who will rescue me from this body of death? (Romans 7:15, 22-24).

That's the Mt. Everest of the Christian life. Sir Edmund Hillary and Tenzing Norgay made the top of their Mt. Everest only because it was the most important thing in the world for them at that moment, regardless of the cost in pain. Honesty—coming into the light, learning reality and the truth about themselves—has always been the most important choice in the world for God's people.

No wonder Revelation calls attention to honesty as one of the unique traits of God's end-time people. They are determined to serve Him and to overcome anything that might prevent them from serving Him, regardless of the cost to themselves in spiritual and emotional pain. The summit—complete victory over everything that separates them from Jesus—is all that matters.

I believe that people with this kind of honesty are to be found in every Christian denomination and in every religion on earth. I also believe that God has had people like this in every generation.

Unique challenges

So why does Revelation make such a point of these honest people in the end time? Because of the unique challenges that this period of history will present. Two factors in particular stand out.

First, the end time will be characterized by unusual deception that will cause people to make terribly wrong choices. Jesus warned that shortly before His return, "false Christs and false prophets will appear and perform great signs and miracles to deceive even the elect—if that were possible" (Matthew 24:24—see also 2 Thessalonians 2:9-12; Revelation 13:13, 14). Only those who have developed a strong internal honesty will be able to withstand the dishonesty in the world around them.

Second, the 144,000 will live during the greatest time of trouble the world has ever known (see Daniel 12:1; Matthew 24:21, 22), and the pressure on them to choose the false teachings and false worship that are rampant in the world will be intense. Will anyone choose to remain loyal to God in the face of this persecution? Yes. Revelation makes it clear that the loyal ones at that time will be those who have climbed the highest mountain of spiritual development and commitment to Jesus, regardless of the cost to themselves.

The point of all this for you and me is quite simple, really: Now is the time for us to be developing the honesty and commitment we will need then. And it's not as difficult as you might think. All you have to do is choose to say one simple prayer and then follow up diligently on whatever answer God gives you. Here's that prayer: "God, show me the things in my life that I need to know in order to be fully committed to You."

The prayer is simple. Choosing to follow up on God's answer may be the most painful thing you or I will ever do. The question that confronts us is this: Will we choose to honestly admit our sin and dysfunction? Will we endure the pain that comes from looking ourselves in the mirror and with God's help deal realistically with what it reveals?

Honesty is the toughest choice we will ever make. But, as Hillary and Norgay—and God's 144,000—will tell you, it's sure great when you reach the top!

1. Sir Edmund Hillary, "The Conquest of the Summit," *National Geographic*, July 1954, 45.

2. Some Bible interpreters believe the number 144,000 is literal, others that it is symbolic. I believe God will have a lot more than 144,000 people on His side at the end of time, so I opt for the symbolic understanding of this number, but the point is not worth arguing over.

3. Revelation 12:17 and 14:12 do not mention the 144,000, but it seems reasonable to assume that they will share the characteristics described in these verses.

4. *People of the Lie* (New York: Touchstone Books, 1985), 82.

5. Ibid., 162.

chapter eight

The Mark of the Beast: A Test of Character

I think I'd have stooped down and tied my shoes—or, in this case, I'd have strapped up my sandals. You can understand, can't you, when the choice was between one of these actions and getting executed? Especially when getting executed meant getting thrown into a fire!

But these fellows, Shadrach, Meshach, and Abednego, didn't strap up their sandals. And they got thrown into a fire. I don't mean they got thrown into the fire for refusing to strap up their sandals. They got thrown into the fire for refusing to kneel down.

Nebuchadnezzar, the king of Babylon, had ordered that an image be set up in a place called the Plain of Dura. Then he had gathered the leading officials of his government and given an order: At the sound of the music, everyone was to fall down and worship the image. Whoever refused would be thrown into a fiery furnace.

But Shadrach, Meshach, and Abednego were Jews as well as public servants—and the second commandment forbids the worship of images. So when the music sounded, these young men chose to stand straight and tall. And God honored their choice by performing a miracle. They were able to walk out of the fire unharmed.

Why do I tell you this story? Because Revelation picks it up as the theme for the second half of chapter 13, which introduces something called "the mark of the beast." Chapter 14 goes on to explain why everyone should avoid getting this mark:

> If anyone worships the beast and his image and receives his mark on the forehead or the hand, he, too, will drink of the wine of God's fury, which has been poured full strength into the cup of his wrath (verses 9, 10).

God's condemnation of those who receive the mark of the beast is one of the most severe found anywhere in the Bible. Accepting the mark of the beast will be absolutely the worst choice a Christian could make. Yet it will be so deceptive that most people will think it is the very best choice to make!

Obviously, it's important to understand what this "mark of the beast" is. Let's find out what Revelation says about it.

The two beasts

Revelation 13 tells about two beasts. The first one rises out of the sea, and the second one rises from the land. These beasts represent two powers that will rule in the world at the end of time. Revelation doesn't name them, but it does tell us what they will do.

Revelation says the sea beast will carry out three significant actions. It will accept worship. "All inhabitants of the earth will worship the beast—all whose names have not been written in the book of life belonging to the Lamb" (verse 8). This is obviously false worship, as is any worship not directed to God.

Accepting worship seems a rather passive "activity." But the other things Revelation says this power will do reveal its true nature. It will blaspheme God and slander His name (verse 6). And it will persecute God's people: it will be "given power to make war against the saints" (verse 7).

The actions of the land beast reveal its nature too. Revelation says it will order the inhabitants of the earth to set up an image in honor of the sea beast, and it will demand the execution of all who refuse to worship the image (verses 14, 15). That's a replay of Nebuchadnezzar's demand that Shadrach, Meshach, and Abednego worship his image or be thrown into the fiery furnace!

Next, Revelation says that the land beast "forced everyone, small and great, rich and poor, free and slave, to receive a mark on his right hand or on his forehead, so that no one could buy or sell unless he had the mark" (verses 16, 17).

If you've heard Christians talk about the mark of the beast and wondered where they got such a phrase, here's where it came from. But the real question is, What does this "mark of the beast" mean?

We will begin to answer this question by examining the setting in which these two beasts carry out their horrible activities. Revelation 12 tells us about a woman and a dragon who are locked in mortal combat. The dragon represents Satan, and the woman represents God's people, so it's really Satan and God's people who are locked in mortal combat.

From the Garden of Eden to the present, Satan has continually attacked God's people, and his purpose has always been to defeat them and if possible, to rid the earth of them. If he had his way, there wouldn't be any followers of God left in the world.

Revelation 12:17 says, "The dragon [Satan] was enraged at the woman [God's people] and went off to make war against the rest of her offspring." When they get really mad at someone, many people will go off somewhere to sulk for a while and plan their revenge. Revelation suggests that Satan went off somewhere to plan his revenge against God's people.

And did he ever plan well! The very next thing we see is the two beasts of Revelation 13 that we've been talking about. They attack God's people. They threaten them with death if they refuse to worship in the politically correct way. And they refuse them the right to buy or sell *unless they receive the mark of the beast.* These beasts confront God's people, and indeed the whole world, with a terrible choice!

That's the setting. Now let's look at the mark itself.

False worship

The first thing to notice is that both the sea beast and the land beast demand worship, just as King Nebuchadnezzar demanded that Shadrach, Meshach, and Abednego engage in worship. Not only that, the two beasts force earth's inhabitants to choose between worshiping in this false way or being killed. Nebuchadnezzar made exactly the same demand of the three Hebrews.

A similar situation also existed during the early days of Christian history. For a time, the official religion of the Roman Empire was emperor worship. During these years, the Roman authorities occasionally stood Christians in front of a pagan altar, handed them a bit of incense, and demanded that they choose between casting the incense onto the altar in worship to the emperor—or being killed.

Is it any wonder that these Christians understood the beast powers of Revelation 13 to represent the Roman Empire and the false worship to involve emperor worship? Perhaps they understood the mark of the beast to be casting incense onto a pagan altar.

Revelation doesn't say what act of worship will be demanded of God's people in the end time. The test that came to Shadrach, Meshach, and Abednego involved kneeling and praying. The possibilities you and I face include singing, praying, preaching, giving offerings, and reading the Bible, to name a few.

While Revelation doesn't say so, I suspect that the choice the world demands of God's people in earth's final days will have two important characteristics: simplicity and visibility. What the king demanded of Shadrach, Meshach, and Abednego was a very simple thing—"Kneel down!" He couldn't make them worship, because that is a mental act that can't be seen. All he could demand was that they perform a simple ritual everyone *could* see.

Whatever form the final test takes, I believe it is reasonable to expect that it will be just as simple and visible as kneeling before a pagan image or casting incense onto a pagan altar.

A matter of character

We must not suppose, however, that the mark of the beast will be a mere outward act. The real issue for Shadrach, Meshach, and Abednego was choosing to remain loyal to God in the face of a challenge by a heathen king. And making that choice was a matter of character.

Please notice this next thought: *Only Christians with very strong characters will choose to stand for their convictions in the face of death during earth's final hours. And the simpler the temptation, the stronger their characters will have to be for them to choose to resist it.* That's because a major part of the temptation will be the thought that it involves such a little thing that choosing to give in won't matter. And Revelation says that those without a character strong enough to resist the temptation will receive the mark of the beast.

Revelation suggests this thought in yet another way. Chapter 12:17, which I quoted earlier, tells us that the remnant of the woman's offspring will "obey God's commandments and hold to the testimony of Jesus." A similar verse appears in chapter 14:12, just after the description of the terrible punishment that will be pronounced on those who receive the mark of the beast. The saints, it says, will "obey God's commandments and remain faithful to Jesus." These Christians will choose to remain loyal to Jesus even during the most vicious attack Satan and the forces of evil have ever brought against God's people! And that loyalty will be manifested by obedience to His commandments.

Now that's character!

If you examine the Ten Commandments carefully (Exodus 20:1-17), you will discover that the first four have to do with our relationship to God and the last six deal with our relationship to other people. Then look carefully at Revelation 13 and

14, and you will discover that each of the first four commandments are implied in these chapters.

The first commandment says, "You shall have no other gods
before me" (Exodus 20:3). The sea beast of Revelation 13 ac-
cepts the worship of people (verses 4, 8), which is a direct violation of this commandment.

The second commandment says, "You shall not make for
yourself an idol in the form of anything in heaven above or on
the earth beneath or in the waters below. You shall not bow
down to them or worship them" (Exodus 20:4, 5). Again, in
direct violation of this clear command from God, the land beast
of Revelation 13 sets up an image to the first beast and then
forces the whole world to worship it (verses 14, 15).

The third commandment says, "You shall not misuse the name
of the Lord your God" (Exodus 20:7), and the sea beast vio-
lates this command. Revelation says that he "opened his mouth
to blaspheme God, and to slander his name" (verse 6).

The fourth commandment

The evidence for the fourth commandment in Revelation 13
and 14 is buried a bit deeper in this passage—but it's there.
Please notice what chapter 14:6, 7 says:

> I saw another angel flying in midair, and he had the
> eternal gospel to proclaim to those who live on the earth—
> to every nation, tribe, language and people. He said in a
> loud voice, "Fear God and give him glory, because the
> hour of his judgment has come. Worship him who made
> the heavens, the earth, the sea and the springs of water."

We need to pay careful attention to two or three things about
these verses. First, they call on God's people to worship Him.
Every other reference to worship in Revelation 13 and 14 has
to do with false worship, but here God calls His people to true
biblical worship.

Now, notice why God's people are to worship Him—because He "made the heavens, the earth, the sea and the springs of water."

Scholars who have made a careful study of Revelation tell us that it contains hundreds of allusions to passages in the Old and New Testaments. They add, however, that not one direct quote from either the Old or New Testament appears anywhere in the entire book. The closest thing to an actual quote is the seven words in chapter 14:7 that I have italicized: "Worship him who *made the heavens, the earth, the sea* and the springs of water."

And where does this "closest thing to an actual quote" come from? From the fourth commandment! Notice the words that I have italicized there: "Remember the Sabbath day by keeping it holy. . . . For in six days the Lord *made the heavens and the earth, the sea*, and all that is in them, but he rested on the seventh day. Therefore the Lord blessed the Sabbath day and made it holy" (Exodus 20:8, 11).[1]

The fourth commandment calls God's people to worship Him as Creator. And in the end time, during the final bitter conflict between the forces of good and evil, God will again call His people to worship Him as Creator—just as the fourth commandment does. In the end time, then, true worship of God will in some way be bound up with the fourth commandment. So it makes sense to suppose that Satan's false worship will in some way involve a false alternative to the Sabbath.

Many Christians today suppose that the disagreement regarding the fourth commandment is simply an argument over which day to go to church—Saturday or Sunday. The day of worship would indeed make an excellent test because it is external and it is both simple and highly visible. But while Seventh-day Adventists affirm that the day is important, the Sabbath encompasses much more. Ultimately, Sabbath keeping means growing in one's relationship with God through spending time with Him. In the end time, some external act will distinguish those who are loyal to God from those who are loyal to Satan. But though that act may involve the matter of Saturday versus Sunday worship, the real issue will be our relationship to God.

Each of us needs to ask ourselves, *What is my relationship to God, to Jesus, today?* Right now, you and I are preparing for the supreme test of our lives. If we live to see the final days of earth's history, then—whether we want to or not—we will face the test over the mark of the beast.

We must begin preparing now for whatever final test God allows to come our way. We need to be sure our choices give God the priority He deserves in our lives.

---

1. Two of the most widely accepted editions of the New Testament in the original Greek language recognize the close relationship between Revelation 14:7 and Exodus 20:11. The *Novum Testamentum Graece,* by Eberhard Nestle, and *The Greek New Testament*, published by the United Bible Societies of London, both cite Exodus 20:11 as a cross reference to Revelation 14:7.

chapter nine

When It Will Be Forever Too Late

Imagine that you are holding a dark bottle in your hand. The bottle has a narrow neck and a fat, ball-shaped bottom. Suddenly, a genie pops out and offers you a choice: During the next year, you can either make twice as much money as you earn now or half as much.

Which would you choose?

Suppose the genie gave you the option of a promotion or a demotion. Which would you choose?

Suppose the genie handed you a cup and said, "Drink the contents, and you will live happily ever after." Would you drink the magic potion, or would you turn it down?

No contest! you say. Who wouldn't choose the extra money, the promotion, and a happy, unending life?

Actually, those choices are not as unlikely as you might think—at least the last one. God offers everyone the opportunity to choose eternal happiness in a land that is far more ideal than anything the balmiest Pacific island could possibly offer.

Now, sometimes free offers and bargain prices require something from those who respond. Some, for instance, come with a time limit on them. To win a lottery, you must buy your tickets before the winning number is chosen. And to benefit from the sale prices at the grocery store or the furniture store, you have to make your purchases before the sale ends.

Similarly, there's a time limit on God's offer of eternal life.

"Wait a minute!" you say. "Surely a loving God wouldn't put a deadline on this offer of His!"

Strange as it may seem, that is exactly what He has done. This is very clear in the Bible, especially in Jesus' parables. I don't mean to suggest that God *wants* to put a time limit on His offer of eternal life, but two factors *require* Him to do so.

The finality of death

The first one is death. Jesus told a parable about a rich farmer who was very foolish. One year this farmer had a bumper crop, so he decided to build huge barns and store the whole crop. That way, he figured, he could retire and live a long, leisurely life. But God said, "You fool! This very night your life will be demanded from you" (Luke 12:20).

Please notice that last sentence: "This very night your life will be demanded from you." These words have a sense of finality to them. Jesus meant that the rich man would die that night and account to God for the way he had chosen to live. It's as if God told the rich man, "The school year has ended, final grades are being passed out, and you flunked." There's not one hint here that God would offer the rich man a chance to live his life over again to see if he could make better choices.

In His parable of the rich man and Lazarus, Jesus expressed even more strongly the finality of the choices we make in this life. In this story a rich man dies, is buried, and ends up in hell. Lazarus, a beggar, also dies—but he ends up by "Abraham's side"—a Jewish figure of speech that meant heaven or eternal life. The rich man begs Abraham to have Lazarus bring him some relief, but he is told that "a great chasm has been fixed, so that those who want to go from here to you cannot, nor can anyone cross over from there to us" (Luke 16:26).

Clearly, Jesus intended us to understand that death fixes a person's eternal destiny forever. There is no changing sides after one dies. All choices for eternity must be made in this life.

The end of the world

The second factor that puts a time limit on God's offer of eternal life is Christ's second coming, which brings about the end of the world. Several of Jesus' parables illustrate this point, including the following:

- The wheat and the weeds (Matthew 13:24-30, 36-43)
- The fish in the net (Matthew 13:47-50)
- The ten virgins (Matthew 25:1-13)
- The men with talents (Matthew 25:14-30)
- The sheep and the goats (Matthew 25:31-46)

Let's examine two of these parables. In the parable of the fish in the net, Jesus said that some fishermen pulled a net filled with fish onto the shore. Then they sorted the fish into two piles—the good fish and the bad fish. "This is how it will be at the end of the age [the second coming]," Jesus explained. "The angels will come and separate the wicked from the righteous and throw them into the fiery furnace, where there will be weeping and gnashing of teeth" (Matthew 13:49-51).

Notice the finality Jesus ascribes to the fate of those who have chosen to reject Him: They will be separated from the righteous and thrown into a fiery furnace. The image of the fiery furnace in Jesus' parable has several implications, one of which is that the wicked will have no second chance to choose eternal life.

This same lesson is taught in Jesus' parable of the sheep and the goats. Jesus began this parable with the words "When the Son of Man comes in his glory, and all the angels with him . . ." These words can refer to only one thing: Jesus' second coming. Jesus went on to say that when He returns, "All the nations will be gathered before him, and he will separate the people one from another as a shepherd separates the sheep from the goats."

In His conclusion to the parable, Jesus said the goats will

"go away to eternal punishment," but the sheep will go "to eternal life" (Matthew 25:46). He didn't give the slightest hint that the wicked would be given a second chance to accept Him and receive eternal life. To the contrary, He specifically said that the wicked will receive *eternal* punishment.

Clearly, God will not, after Christ's second coming, offer a second chance at eternal life to those who rejected the offer before Christ's return. All choices concerning our eternal destiny must be made in this life. Any later will be too late.

The close of probation

Christians sometimes use the term *probationary time* to refer to the period during which human beings have the opportunity to accept Jesus and be saved or to reject Him and be lost. And the end of probationary time is called "the close of probation."

The following words in Revelation make it clear that probation *will* close someday: "He that is unjust, let him be unjust still: and he which is filthy, let him be filthy still: and he that is righteous, let him be righteous still: and he that is holy, let him be holy still" (Revelation 22:11, KJV). This verse says that one day, the final choice of each human being will become his or her eternal choice.

Those who die before Jesus comes will have their whole lives to accept or reject Him, because God will wait till they die to pass final judgment on them. In other words, their probation will not end until they die. However, the probation of those who are still alive when Jesus comes—their opportunity to accept or reject God's offer of eternal life—will end *before* they die. God will pass final judgment on them while they are still alive.

If probation is going to close someday, finalizing all choices for and against God, then it's extremely important that we know when this will happen so we can be sure to be ready. Jesus' parables suggest that people will be able to accept or reject God right up to His second coming (see figure 1). In one of these parables, for example, the separation of the righteous and the wicked into two classes takes place "at the end of the age"; in another, it occurs "when the Son of Man comes in his glory" (Matthew 13:49; 25:31).

Revelation, however, suggests a slightly different scenario.

The close of probation in Revelation

Both Jesus and Revelation assure us that the human race will be divided into just two classes at the end of time: the righteous and the wicked. Jesus illustrated this with His figures of the wheat and the weeds, the good and the bad fish, the wise and the foolish virgins, and the sheep and the goats. Revelation uses these same two categories when it says the righteous will receive the seal of God and the wicked will receive the mark of the beast.[1]

As to when this division will take place, as we have seen, Jesus' parables suggest that it will occur *at* the second coming of Christ. However, according to Revelation, it will occur *before* Christ's second coming. The evidence is really quite simple to understand, but first we need a bit of background about the seven last plagues. (These plagues are described in Revelation 16. You might find it helpful to read that chapter before continuing with this article.)

All the seven last plagues will occur before the second coming of Christ. That being the case, the first plague will occur quite some time before the second coming. And notice who Revelation says will suffer the effects of the first plague:

> The first angel went and poured out his bowl on the land, and ugly and painful sores broke out on the people *who had the mark of the beast and worshiped his image* (Revelation 16:2).

The important point to notice here is that the first plague will fall only on those who have received the mark of the beast—that is, the wicked. Obviously, then, the final determination of who receives the mark of the beast and who receives the seal of God will have to be made before the first plague is poured out. Since the seven last plagues will fall only on the wicked, and since these plagues will occur before the second coming of Christ, it is evident that the close of probation—each human being's final decision for or against God—must also take place *before* the second coming of Christ and not *at* His coming.[2]

So, during the seven last plagues, those who have made a final choice for God will live on the earth together with those who have chosen irrevocably to reject Him. However, the two groups will not be physically separated until Christ's second coming, as Jesus taught in His parables.[3]

We close our own probation

Does it still seem unfair to you that at some point in the future, God will cut off the opportunity to accept Him and obtain eternal life? Actually, we will cut off that opportunity ourselves.

If you read the preceding chapter, you know that the mark of the beast and the seal of God are tests of character. God never forces upon us the choices that form our characters. We are completely free to make those choices ourselves. However, God will not shield us from the unfortunate consequences of our wrong choices. If by our choices we form a character that is opposed to God and His way of life, the dramatic events just before Jesus comes will reveal that.

Earlier I quoted the verse from Revelation that says, "He that is unjust, let him be unjust still: . . . and he that is holy, let him be holy still." God is not telling us here about something He will do to us. He is acknowledging what we will have done to ourselves.

The biblical teaching about the close of probation is extremely important for you and me to understand at the present time. While the second coming of Jesus will be an earth-shattering event that every human being will be aware of, only God will know when every human being has made his or her final choice. Thus God alone will know when probation closes.[4] We must be ready at all times. That's why Jesus said, "Therefore keep watch, because you do not know the day or the hour" (Matthew 25:13).

I cannot say strongly enough that the time to choose God is *now*. The time to accept Jesus as your Saviour and so to obtain forgiveness of your sins is *now*. The time to choose the transformation of heart and the cleansing from sin that Jesus offers is *now*.

---

1. The seal of God is described in Revelation 7:1-4; 14:1-5. The mark of the beast is described in Revelation 13:16, 17; 14:9-11; 16:1.

2. Actually, the seventh plague *is* the second coming of Christ. This is evident when we compare Revelation 6:12-17, which clearly is a description of the second coming, with the seventh plague in chapter 16:17-21. Chapter 6 tells us that at Christ's second coming an earthquake will occur that is so powerful that "every mountain and island [will be] removed from its place" (verse 14). This same imagery is used in connection with the seventh plague (see Revelation 16:18, 20), making it clear that the seventh plague is identical to the second coming of Christ. So the previous six plagues, including the first one, must occur *before* the second coming of Christ.

3. Regarding the relationship between the close of probation and the second coming, Jesus' parables only *seem* to differ from Revelation. The Bible uses many terms to refer to the end of the world, terms like the *day of the Lord* and the *end of the age*. Often, those who used these terms had in mind the whole complex of events related to that climax; at the moment, they weren't concerned with laying out all the details. In other words, their terms included the close of probation, the seven last plagues, the second coming, and more—without specifying the sequence or relationship in time. Jesus' parables paint this kind of a broad picture.

4. Presumably, the angels will know when human probation has closed.

chapter ten

A Good and Angry God

Does God get angry?

That was the topic of discussion in a Bible-study class I attended recently. Some class members said Yes; others said No.

"God is loving and kind," said those who didn't want an angry God. The other side countered with Bible passages that describe a God of wrath.

After a few moments, I turned to a friend I'll call Harry, who is the father of two teenage daughters. "How would you feel," I said, "if you came home one evening and found an intruder assaulting one of your daughters?"

Harry looked at me with a puzzled expression on his face, and then he said, "Murderous."

"And how would you want God to feel?" I asked.

"Murderous," he said.

"In other words," I replied, "you would want a God who was just as angry about what was happening as you were."

"That's right," he said.

I've been party to a number of discussions about God's love and His anger in the past few years, and I've noticed that almost without exception they end up at an impasse. Both sides seem to ignore a fundamental fact of human existence: Love and anger are not opposites. They are complementary. Only those who are capable of feeling genuine anger can love in the truest sense.

It's the parents with the greatest love for their children who will do the most to save them from abuse. And it's anger that will fuel their actions. Without anger, we would watch abuse and fail to understand the seriousness of what was happening.

Actually, millions of people long for an angry God. "Where was God when my child got hit by a car?" they demand. "Where was God when I lost my job?" "Where was God when I got cancer?"

Why have I focused in so closely on anger and love? Because we have to be clear about this relationship before we can understand the most terrible description of God's wrath found anywhere in the Bible. Please notice the following passage from Revelation:

> If anyone worships the beast and his image and receives his mark on the forehead or on the hand, he, too, will drink of the wine of God's fury, which has been poured full strength into the cup of his wrath. He will be tormented with burning sulfur in the presence of the holy angels and of the Lamb (Revelation 14:9, 10).

The terrible wrath of God that this passage warns against consists of seven horrible plagues that will fall upon the human race during the final days of earth's history, just before Jesus comes. Revelation introduces these plagues with the following words: "Then I heard a loud voice from the temple saying to the seven angels, 'Go, pour out the seven bowls of God's wrath on the earth' " (Revelation 16:1).

I want to state clearly that I believe absolutely in a God of love. The Bible says that God doesn't want anyone to die (see 2 Peter 3:9). It tells of a God who "so loved the world that he gave his one and only Son" to die that you and I might live (John 3:16). "God," the Bible says, "is love" (1 John 4:8).

But how should a loving God respond when human beings abuse each other? How, for instance, should God respond to

Auschwitz? If the Nuremberg trial was justified—and I believe most people agree that it was—then before we judge God too harshly for the seven last plagues, we need to ask whether the people upon whom they will fall truly deserve them.

Let's answer that question by examining the context of the plagues—both the broad historical context and the immediate context in which the plagues themselves occur.

The historical context

The Bible says that war broke out in heaven thousands of years ago, when Satan rebelled against God. "Michael and his angels fought against the dragon [Satan], and the dragon and his angels fought back" (Revelation 12:7). Revelation adds that "the great dragon was hurled . . . to the earth, and his angels with him" (verse 9).

God never planned for our world to be the place of suffering that you and I know today. But when Satan and his angels arrived on our planet, they enticed our first parents to join them in their rebellion against God (see Genesis 3:1-6). Adam and Eve chose to reject God and accept Satan! And because of their choice and similar choices people have been making ever since, the history of our world is filled with tales of terrible evil.

God hates evil because of the suffering it brings to human beings. Auschwitz may be the world's most terrible example of this suffering, but it is hardly the only one. Every murder, every robbery, every case of child abuse, is a reminder of that evil. And it is in precisely these situations that we humans *want* an angry God who will *do* something about this awful suffering.

Because God has chosen not to end evil during our short lifetimes, it's easy to assume that He has no plan for dealing with it at all. But Revelation assures us that He will bring suffering and sin to an end. The seven last plagues are an important part of His plan.

Satan isn't happy about God's intention, of course. He's the author of sin, and he wants sin to continue because that's the only way he can maintain his power over the world. So he intends to fight God to the bitter end.

Satan's effort at the end of time to hold onto his power brings us to the second part of the background that we need to know to understand the terrible wrath of God in the seven last plagues.

The immediate context

Revelation makes it clear that Satan will launch fierce attacks against God's people during earth's final days. Chapter 12:17 says "the dragon [Satan] was enraged at the woman [God's people] and went off to make war against the rest of her offspring."

Revelation 13 gives us even more detail. It describes an end-time power that will rebel against God. And notice what it will do: "He was given power to make war against the saints and to conquer them" (verse 7).

Later in chapter 13 we discover another beast with murderous intentions, one that will actually threaten to kill anyone who refuses to worship in the politically correct way (verse 15)! And chapter 17 describes an evil woman who will be "drunk with the blood of the saints, the blood of those who bore testimony to Jesus" (verse 6).

That sounds an awful lot like the Holocaust to me! So how should God respond?

It's time to take another look at the seven last plagues.

The seven last plagues

The third plague is especially relevant to what we've been talking about. In this plague, the rivers and springs of water become blood (see Revelation 16:4). Immediately, an angel from heaven comments:

> You are just in these judgments, . . .
> *for they have shed the blood of your saints and prophets,*

and you have given them blood to drink as they de-
serve (verses 5, 6).

Notice that God allows these terrible judgments to happen[1]
because the people on whom they fall have been abusing His
saints! *Suddenly, the wrath of God in the seven last plagues*
begins to make sense.

I suspect that to a large degree, we have a hard time with the
idea of an angry God because of all the bad examples of anger
we've seen. To most of us, anger means temper tantrums and
pouting. If that's genuine anger, then yes, please, spare me an
angry God.

That's the kind of anger the gods of the heathen have—they
hold grudges and vent their wrath capriciously on anyone who
happens to get in their way. But the wrath of God that's described in the Bible, and especially in Revelation, serves to rid
the world of the sin and suffering that evil causes.

The good news for Christians

The book of Revelation seems filled with doom and gloom,
doesn't it? It's true that Revelation says a lot about fire and
brimstone and the wrath of God. Yet viewed properly, God's
wrath offers tremendous hope for Christians.

Go back a few chapters with me to Revelation 6:10. This
passage pictures the souls of martyrs under an altar. Notice
what they say: "How long, Sovereign Lord, holy and true,
until you judge the inhabitants of the earth and avenge our
blood?" These people are desperate for a God who will get
worked up enough—angry enough, if you please—over the
abuse they've been suffering that He'll step in and *do* something about it!

The seven last plagues are good news to the martyrs!

The martyrs paid the ultimate price because of the choice
they made to stand for their faith. You and I may not be called
to make that ultimate choice, but the seven last plagues are

good news to us too. They're good news because we live in a world that is saturated with immorality, crime, and terrorism.

Have you ever wondered how much longer God will allow this condition to go on? I have.

The seven last plagues are good news because they tell those who live when these plagues fall that God is about to end the reign of sin.

But Satan isn't about to just lie down and die. He'll resist God's plan to the bitter end.

Admittedly, the final war between good and evil isn't going to be any more pleasant to live through than World War II was for Europeans. Yet for all its horror, that conflict was good news because it preserved freedom in the world.

Similarly, for all its horror, the final conflict between good and evil is good news for God's people because it will make possible a world free of the sin and suffering that we endure today.

One additional bit of information about the seven last plagues is particularly good news: These plagues will fall on the wicked only, not on God's people. While God's people will suffer as a result of the conflict, God will be on their side, protecting them. I believe that the promises in Psalm 91 apply especially to God's people during the seven last plagues:

> He who dwells in the shelter of the Most High
>   will rest in the shadow of the Almighty.
> I will say of the Lord, "He is my refuge and my fortress,
>   my God, in whom I trust."
> Surely he will save you from the fowler's snare
>   and from the deadly pestilence.
> He will cover you with his feathers,
>   and under his wings you will find refuge. . . .
> A thousand may fall at your side,
>   ten thousand at your right hand,
>   but it will not come near you.

You will only observe with your eyes
    and see the punishment of the wicked
                (verses 1-8).

That's got to be good news for us—who know that as Christians, we may have to live through the seven last plagues someday. And one other bit of good news: The same psalm that promises us deliverance from the plagues also tells how we can be assured of that protection:

If you make the Most High your dwelling—
    even the Lord, who is my refuge—
then no harm will befall you,
    no disaster will come near your tent
                (verses 9, 10).

Here, then, is another of Revelation's choices. No one need suffer the seven last plagues. Whether or not we do depends on whether or not we choose to make the Most High our "dwelling"—whether or not we place our lives and our fate in His hands before those plagues begin to fall.

---

1. The language of Revelation 16 suggests that God actually causes the seven last plagues to fall on the wicked. Some Christians explain this by saying that God withholds His protection, allowing Satan and the forces of nature to cause them. At the very least, we can say that God is responsible for the seven last plagues in that He has it within His power to prevent them but does not do so.

The Seven Last Plagues

Number	Where poured out	Effect
First	On the land	People who have the mark of the beast develop painful sores.
Second	On the sea	The sea becomes blood, and all marine life dies.
Third	On the rivers and springs of water	All the sources of fresh water produce blood instead.
Fourth	On the sun	The sun scorches people, and they curse God.
Fifth	On the throne	People gnaw their tongues in agony, and they curse God.
Sixth	On the river	The water in the river is dried up to prepare the way for the kings from the East.
Seventh	On the air	A voice from the temple says, "It is done!" and huge hailstones fall to the earth.

chapter eleven

Invasion From Outer Space

Pretend for a moment that you're a Hollywood film producer. Currently, you're creating a science-fiction space odyssey about a race of beings from a distant part of the universe that is intent on invading planet Earth and destroying it. The leader of the alien race is a powerful potentate who has mastered the forces of nature and can use them at any time to enforce his will.

The world's leaders have been hopelessly divided. But when they become aware of the approaching threat, they quickly set aside their differences and begin to plan a united defense. One of their major concerns is that a few of earth's inhabitants are loyal to the enemy. The world's leaders quickly round up the majority of these dissidents, throw them in prison, and threaten to execute any who refuse to submit to the allied cause. The few who remain free go into deep hiding.

Contrary to conventional wisdom, you decide that your film will take the side of the invaders and earth's dissident minority. The aliens will defeat the allied forces, rescue the prisoners and fugitives, and destroy the planet.

As you develop the scenario, you have to plot the alien race's strategy for invading the planet. You could have them enter earth space secretly and take the world's leaders by surprise. But since your alien potentate holds such absolute control over the forces of nature, you decide to have him confront the human race openly with a powerful show of force right from the start. He and all his warriors will ride across the sky, where everyone can see them. Their powerful laser beams will send every human being bolting for cover.

The potentate's warriors will release all their human friends from their prison cells and hiding places. They'll escort them to the alien spaceship and triumphantly whisk them away to their planet in a distant galaxy, where everyone will live happily ever after.

Does this plot sound interesting? It should. It was created by the greatest Producer of all time—though He hasn't brought it to life yet. Amazingly, the story isn't science fiction. In fact, it originated in the Bible; Revelation describes it quite in detail.

It's called "the second coming of Christ."

Pictures of the invasion

Revelation gives us four word pictures of Christ's return. Let's see how they describe His "invasion from outer space."

Revelation 1:7

The alien Potentate, of course, is Jesus Christ, who truly does control all the forces of nature. We find a brief description of His bold approach to planet Earth in the very first chapter of Revelation: "Look, he is coming with the clouds, and every eye will see him, even those who pierced him; and all the peoples of the earth will mourn because of him" (verse 7).

Coming "with the clouds" so that "every eye will see him" is identical to the strategy of our fictional invaders from outer space. Jesus will confront earth's inhabitants openly, boldly riding through the sky with a powerful show of force.

And notice the response of the human race: They will mourn. Why? Because they've missed out on the "living happily ever after" ending to this story.

The Bible consistently points to the second coming of Christ as the transition point between this life and the next. Speaking of Christ's return, Paul said that then will "the mortal [be clothed] with immortality," and then will we "be with the Lord forever" (1 Corinthians 15:53; 1 Thessalonians 4:17). The people who mourn at Christ's second coming will grieve because they had the opportunity to have eternal life but chose to turn it down.

Revelation 6:12-17

Let's go back to that Hollywood film you are producing. Knowing that the right backdrop can add a powerful emotional impact to a scene, you are anxious to make the sky look just right. You decide to have your alien potentate block out the sun with a worldwide cover of dark, ominous clouds. A blood-red moon will show through a break in the clouds. And to complete the scene, your potentate will bring on a meteorite shower and several asteroids that become balls of fire as they plunge toward the earth.

Again, that's exactly how Revelation describes Christ's second coming: "The sun turned black like sackcloth made of goat hair, the whole moon turned blood red, and the stars in the sky fell to earth" (chapter 6:12, 13).

You'll want your potentate to show people his power, of course. What better way than to have him shift the planet on its axis, creating a powerful earthquake that sets the planet's tectonic plates crashing into each other?

Revelation speaks of an earthquake so powerful that it moves every mountain and island from its place. Imagine the Rocky Mountains moving over to displace the Allegheny Mountains! That sounds like about a thousand on the Richter Scale![1]

How would your alien potentate want his foes to respond to his bold ride across the sky? He couldn't ask for anything better than what Revelation describes: "The kings of the earth, the princes, the generals, the rich, the mighty, and every slave and every free man hid in caves and among the rocks of the mountains. They called to the mountains and the rocks, 'Fall on us and hide us from the face of him who sits on the throne and from the wrath of the Lamb!' " (verses 15, 16).

This is mass suicide! Can you imagine nearly all the human race committing suicide at once? Jonestown was child's play compared to this!

Why do these people want to die? Because they'll have seen God face to face. All their lives, atheists have challenged God: "If You exist, show Yourself to us, and we'll believe in You!" Now they'll see. And they'll be filled with such terror that they'll want to die.

Revelation 14:14-20

Revelation's third word picture is based on a "harvest" theme; it portrays Jesus seated on a cloud (again) and holding a sickle, which is a tool for harvesting grain. We don't usually think of an alien invasion as a harvest, but let's see what this passage says that might be useful for our space-age motion picture.

This harvest is portrayed as having two stages. In the first, Jesus swings the sickle and does the reaping. This part of the harvest represents the salvation of God's people; the alien warriors whisk their loyal friends from captivity on this earth to freedom on their "planet in a distant galaxy." The rescuees will come from two groups: those who have died and are resurrected at Christ's coming and those who have lived to see Him come.

Revelation devotes even more space to its description of the second part of the harvest—that of the wicked. "Another angel came out of the temple in heaven," it says, "and he too had a sharp sickle. . . . The angel swung his sickle on the earth, gathered its grapes and threw them into the great winepress of God's wrath" (chapter 14:17-19). The fact that these people suffer the wrath of God is clear evidence that they are His enemies.

But what really catches your eye as a film producer is the final image in this part of Revelation. Verse 20 says that after the grapes are thrown into the winepress, "blood flowed out the press, rising as high as the horses' bridles for a distance of 1,600 stadia" (about 180 miles).

How are you going to create that scene on film? The language is symbolic, of course. The vast amount of blood suggests death on an incredible scale. It means that all those who are in rebellion against God will die when Jesus comes.

Revelation 19:11-21

A moment ago, we had our alien potentate riding across the sky on a cloud. Now imagine him riding a huge white horse. An enormous army of alien warriors follows him, each on his own white horse.

War dominates Revelation's final picture of Jesus' coming: "I saw heaven standing open and there before me was a white horse, whose rider is called Faithful and True. . . . Out of his mouth comes a sharp sword with which to strike down the nations. . . . The armies of heaven were following him, riding on white horses and dressed in fine linen" (chapter 19:11, 15, 14).

In war, nations aim to break the power of their foes. That's exactly what Jesus will do when He comes back to planet Earth. He will "strike down the nations"; He will destroy all of earth's governments.

It's hard to imagine a world without a United States or a Canada, isn't it? No Germany, no China, no Japan. So who's going to rule over all the people?

The answer to that question may surprise you: No one will— because there won't be anyone left on earth to be ruled. Revelation's next few verses make it very clear that when Jesus and His faithful followers leave this world to go to heaven,[2] the wicked will all be dead. No human beings will be left alive on planet Earth.

Revelation shows us an angel standing in the sun and crying to all the birds of the air, "Come, gather together for the great supper of God, so that you may eat the flesh of kings, generals, and mighty men, of horses and their riders, and the flesh of all people, free and slave, small and great" (verses 17, 18).

The birds described here eat carrion—the flesh of the dead. This is Revelation's symbolic way of telling us that the wicked will all die at Christ's coming.

Verses 19 to 21 reinforce this point. Verse 19 shows "the kings of the earth and their armies gathered together to make war against the rider on the horse and his army." Can't you picture the world's greatest military leaders training their nuclear warheads on an incoming alien invasion? But they will lose the war. Verse 21 says that they will be "killed with the sword that came out of the mouth of the rider on the horse [Jesus], and all the birds [will gorge] themselves on their flesh."

What it all means

Jesus' second coming will indeed be an "invasion from outer space." Above all else, Revelation is telling us that the world as we know it is going to end someday. Everything that is familiar to you and me will be totally destroyed. Our planet will become a huge pile of rubble.

Why would a good God want to wreak such destruction on the world He created several thousand years ago? Because the world He'll find when He returns will differ so vastly from the one He created. God gave us a pristine planet. We've turned it into an ecological cesspool. He created human beings noble and happy. We've turned ourselves into raving maniacs.

The pictures I've seen of Christ's second coming usually show a father, mother, and children welcoming Him with outstretched arms. That's a good image of Christ's coming. You'll find strong support for it in Bible verses like Luke 21:28 and 1 Thessalonians 4:13-18.

However, because Revelation is primarily concerned with the conflict between good and evil, it naturally describes Christ's return in the stark terms of armies marshaling for battle, of terrible natural disasters (God's weapons), of conquest and defeat. This sounds bad to us, because we don't like war. But

God's final war is good news for those who have chosen to place their faith in Jesus Christ, because it signals their deliverance from the evil forces that are running loose in the world.

The conflict between good and evil is going on right now—both in our world and in the heart of each of us. But Jesus truly does plan on rescuing every one of His faithful followers from planet Earth, and I believe this will happen in the very near future.

Fortunately, there is still time to choose God, to join His side.

---

1. Shifting the earth on its axis is one way among several that God might cause the great earthquake that will take place at Christ's coming.

2. Before He left the earth two thousand years ago, Jesus told His followers that He was going to His Father's house in heaven to prepare a place for them. "I will come back," He said, "and take you to be with me that you also may be where I am" (John 14:3). Clearly, at His second coming, Jesus will take His people to be with Him in heaven.

Putting Satan in His Place

A thousand years ago, Europe was awash in speculations about the end of the first millennium A.D. "The whole of Europe was seized with a paroxysm of preapocalyptic shivers," said one author, commenting on that period of history.[1]

And another wrote, "The number 1000 oppressed Europe like a nightmare. A wave of fatalism seized the people: the great cataclysm was about to engulf the world. . . . Whole towns repaired to church as one man, or assembled round crucifixes under the open sky, there to await God's judgment on corporately bended knees."[2]

A similar spasm of millennial fever grips the world as we approach the end of the second millennium A.D. Forecasts for the year 2000 include everything from a worldwide earthquake caused by the globe shifting on its axis to the dawn of a glorious age of peace. Various Protestant groups are aiming to evangelize the world by the turn of the millennium, and John Paul talks openly of a major jubilee celebration in the year 2000, possibly in the nation of Israel.

With the growing frenzy about the millennium and the year 2000, perhaps it's time that we took a look at what the Bible says about millenniums—specifically, *the* millennium.

The word *millennium* means "one thousand years."[3] The religious concept of a millennium that is an important part of the biblical end-time scenario comes from the twentieth chapter of Revelation. If you believe, as I do, that the Bible is God's Word, then whatever others may say about the millennium, for you, the Bible is the most authoritative source of information about this important subject. In this chapter we're going to look at what Revelation says about the millennium and the events immediately after it.

For those who've never read it before, Revelation's description of the millennium may seem confusing. The key to figuring it all out is to understand that John divides his comments into three parts, each part ending with what Revelation calls a "lake of burning sulfur" (verse 10) or a "lake of fire" (verses 14, 15).

The first part (chapter 20:1-10) is the only one in which John discusses the entire millennium. The second and third parts (chapters 20:11-21:1 and 21:2-8) focus on events at the end of the millennium, and each of these parts has a different emphasis. (Figure 1 diagrams these three parts of John's discussion.)

Let's take a closer look at each of these descriptions.

The first description

John begins his first—and most complete—description of the millennium with these words:

> I saw an angel coming down out of heaven, having the key to the Abyss and holding in his hand a great chain. He seized the dragon, that ancient serpent, who is the devil, or Satan, and bound him for a thousand years. He threw him into the Abyss, and locked and sealed it over him, to keep him from deceiving the nations anymore until the thousand years were ended. After that, he must be set free for a short time (Revelation 20:1, 2).

In the English language, the word *abyss* means "a chasm" or "a deep fissure in the earth." But since Revelation is filled with symbolic language, we probably shouldn't think John meant that Satan will be bound with a literal chain or that he will be thrown into a literal chasm.

The same Greek word—*abyss*—used in Revelation 20 is used in Genesis 1:2 to describe the condition of the world before God made it into the earth we know today. There, this word means "formless and empty."[4] This is probably an accurate description of the shape planet Earth will be in after the devastation that will occur at Christ's second coming and the severe judgments of God that lead up to it.

Revelation, then, seems to be telling us that Satan will be bound or confined to this earth during the millennium.

But the question about the millennium that I'd guess is most on people's minds these days is, When will the millennium begin?

Revelation is quite clear on that. It says that God's people "came to life and reigned with Christ a thousand years" (verse 4). The expression "came to life" refers to the resurrection, which will occur at Christ's second coming (see 1 Corinthians 15:51-53; 1 Thessalonians 4:13-18). Clearly, then, the millennium will begin at Christ's second coming.

Perhaps you noticed that Revelation also says that God's people will reign with Christ during the thousand years. Where will they reign with Him?

Some Christians believe that Christ and His people will rule over the wicked on the earth during the millennium. There are at least two reasons why this cannot be true.

First, the Bible makes it very clear that the righteous and the wicked will be separated from each other at the second coming of Christ. In Matthew 25:31, for example, Jesus said, "When the Son of Man comes in his glory, and all the angels with him [Christ's second coming], . . . he will separate the people one from another as a shepherd separates the sheep from the goats."

If you will read Jesus' entire parable (verses 31-46), you will see that the sheep represent God's people and the goats represent the wicked. Jesus made it absolutely clear that the righteous and the wicked will be separated from each other at His second coming.

The second reason why the righteous cannot rule over the wicked during the millennium is that the righteous will be in heaven and the wicked will be dead upon the earth. Let's see what the Bible has to say about where the righteous and the wicked end up after the second coming.

Shortly before He left this earth, Jesus told His disciples that He would soon be returning to His Father's house (heaven) to prepare a place for them. Then He assured them, "If I go and prepare a place for you, I will come back and take you to be with me that you also may be where I am" (John 14:1-3).

Jesus is in heaven right now, of course, preparing a place for us, just as He promised (see Hebrews 8:1, 2). And when He comes back, He will take us to heaven to be with Him. That's what He said He is going to do.

But will all the wicked really be dead during that time? Let's examine the evidence for that idea.

In 2 Thessalonians 1:7, 8, Paul said that at Christ's second coming the wicked will be "punished with everlasting destruction." Revelation 19:17-21 says the same thing in symbolic language. In these verses an angel calls the birds of the air to feast on the bodies of the wicked, who attack Christ at His second coming. Verse 21 says clearly that the wicked "were killed with the sword that came out of the mouth of the rider on the horse, and all the birds gorged themselves on their flesh."

These and similar passages in the Bible help us to understand that the wicked will indeed be dead during the millennium. So even if the righteous were to be alive on the earth during that time, they could not rule over the wicked. Nor can Satan, even though he is bound to the earth during the thousand years. Did you notice that Revelation 20 says that Satan won't deceive the nations during the millennium (verse 3)? He can't! With the righteous in heaven and the wicked all dead, there won't be anyone for him to deceive.

Revelation says that at the end of the millennium, Satan will be released from the great abyss where he was bound for a thousand years (verse 7). And at that time, his wicked followers will be resurrected.[5] The loosing of Satan does not mean he will be free to roam the universe beyond planet Earth. He will only be free to deceive the nations of earth again—because they're alive again and accessible to him.

Satan will take charge of all the wicked human beings who ever lived, who "in number [are] like the sand on the seashore" (verse 8). Revelation says they will march "across the breadth of the earth" and surround "the camp of God's people, the city he loves." But then fire comes down from heaven and devours them (verse 9).

What is this "camp of God's people, the city he loves"? If God's people are in heaven during the millennium, how can their "camp," or their city, be on the earth at the end of the millennium? Please hold these questions for just a few moments.

The second description

You will recall that Revelation's second and third descriptions deal exclusively with events at the end of the millennium. The second description is found in Revelation 20:11–21:1. John tells us that he saw "a great white throne and him who was seated on it. Earth and sky fled from his presence" (verse 11). The One seated on the throne is obviously God.

Verse 12 says that all the dead stand before the throne. These people are the wicked of all ages, who were resurrected at the end of the thousand years (see verse 5) and so are not literally dead at this point. Now we see why they were raised to life at the end of the millennium: for judgment. Revelation says that heaven's ledger books—the record of all the deeds of all human beings—will be opened at this time.

But why will God wait till after the millennium to judge the wicked? Did He not judge them before Christ's second coming so that He would know whom to save and whom to punish?

Of course He did. This judgment will not be for God's benefit but for that of the rest of the universe. Romans 14:11 promises us that someday "every knee will bow before me [God]; every tongue will confess to God." There has never been a time when God's people did not praise Him, but throughout history, the wicked have gone to their graves without praising Him. They will praise Him after the millennium, though, for the judgment at that time will show them just where their lives went astray and why they must stand forever condemned. This realization will wring an acknowledgment of God's justice from their lips—which will add further confirmation to the faith of the rest of the inhabitants of the universe of the goodness of God.

Revelation says that following the final judgment, the wicked will be cast into the lake of fire. Notice that "death and Hades [the grave]" (verse 14) will also be cast into the lake of fire.

Fortunately, Revelation's second description of events after the millennium concludes on a happier note than that of the lake of fire. Revelation 21:1 says, "Then I saw a new heaven and a new earth, for the first heaven and the first earth had passed away, and there was no longer any sea."

So Revelation tells us the final fate of both the righteous and the wicked. The wicked will be destroyed in the lake of fire, and the righteous will live forever on a recreated earth. (I will discuss both the lake of fire [or hell] and the new earth with you in much greater detail in the concluding chapters of this book, so I will not say anything more about them here.)

The third description

Now let's return to the question of this "camp of the saints, the city he loves." In Revelation 21:2, John writes, "I saw the Holy City, the new Jerusalem, coming down out of heaven from God." Since it follows the description of the re-creation of the earth in verse 1, it would appear at first glance that this descent of the city will happen after God has re-created the earth.

However, in chapter 20:9 we saw "the city [God] loves" on

the earth for the wicked to attack after their resurrection and before they are cast into the lake of fire. This city that God loves has to be the New Jerusalem. So Revelation 21:2 backs us up to describe from yet another angle those events that will occur immediately after the millennium—events that will lead up to the lake of fire.

But these verses in chapter 21 focus primarily on the righteous. God promises His followers that in contrast to the fate of the wicked—who will be cast into the lake of fire (verse 8)—He will be their God forever (verse 3). They will never again be sick or suffer or die (verse 4).

In Revelation, then, God promises us that a day is coming when all the pain and heartache of this life will be over. Never again will insane people blow up buildings with bombs. Never again will demented rulers start wars that kill thousands and sometimes millions of innocent people. In that world we will never go through the pain of divorce, never suffer from accidents or crippling diseases, never attend another funeral.

Revelation's word picture of the millennium shows us the final result of the choices you and I are making right now. Our choices today are determining our destiny then—whether we will be part of God's plans for a renewed paradise or shut out of that world for ever and ever and ever.

---

1. Bill Lawren, "Apocalypse Now," *Psychology Today,* May 1989, 41; cited in Russell Chandler, *Doomsday: The End of the World* (Ann Arbor, Mich.: Servant Publications, 1989), 48.

2. Richard Lewinsohn, *Science, Prophecy, and Prediction* (New York: Bell, 1961), 78; cited in Chandler.

3. From two Latin words: *mille,* which means "one thousand," and *annum,* which means "year."

4. The Old Testament was written in Hebrew. When it was translated into the Greek language, the translators chose the word *abyss* to express the idea of "formless and empty" in Genesis 1:2.

5. Revelation says "the rest of the dead did not come to life until the thousand years were ended." Since the righteous were raised at the beginning of the millennium, the words "the rest of the dead" have to refer to the wicked.

Figure 1

The Three Parts of John's Description of the Millennium

First description

1,000 years (the millennium)	End of the millennium
Revelation 20:1-10	

Second description

	End of the millennium
Focus on the wicked ————→	Rev. 20:11–21:1

Third description

	End of the millennium
Focus on the righteous ————→	Rev. 21:2-8

The Millennium: What and When

Beginning of the millennium
    Second coming of Christ
    Resurrection of the righteous
    Destruction of the wicked
    Righteous taken to heaven
    Earth destroyed by an earthquake
    Satan bound to the desolate earth

During the millennium
    Righteous in heaven
    Wicked dead on the earth
    Satan bound to the earth

End of the millennium
    New Jerusalem descends from heaven to earth
    Resurrection of the wicked
    Satan loosed
    Satan and the wicked attack the New Jerusalem
    Great white throne judgment
    Lake of fire

Earth recreated, eternity begins

chapter thirteen

When God Destroys Sin

"A long time ago, in a galaxy far, far away . . ." So read the opening words of *Star Wars*, the first of a popular line of fictional space odysseys.

In the film, Ben Kenobi and Luke Skywalker are among the last survivors of a race of good warriors called the Jedi. An Evil Empire has destroyed their planet, massacred the rest of the Jedi, and is seeking to kill Ben and Luke. In due time the pair find themselves trapped with their friends inside the Evil Empire's monster spaceship. In a hand-to-hand fight with Darth Vader, the sinister leader of the Evil Empire, Ben Kenobi sacrifices his life, making it possible for Luke Skywalker and the remaining Jedi to escape.

Luke Skywalker and his companions are not safe, though, because warriors of the Evil Empire take after them in hot pursuit. Then, from a base on a distant planet, Luke Skywalker attacks the Evil Empire's spaceship at its one vulnerable point and destroys it, ending the drama.

The most striking aspect of *Star Wars* is the close similarity between the film and the conflict between good and evil that has been going on in the universe for thousands of years. We all know that *Star Wars* is fictional. But the Bible tells us that a very real war broke out a long time ago, in a "galaxy far, far away"—called heaven.

"Michael and his angels fought against the dragon, and the dragon and his angels fought back," is how Revelation describes this war (chapter 12:7). The hostilities began when Satan, the "dragon," rebelled against God's government. Fortunately, God's forces were stronger, and Satan and his angels were cast out of heaven. Unfortunately for you and me, they were cast onto planet Earth. Ever since, our world has been the site of the conflict between good and evil.

This conflict between God and Satan is moral—so when our first parents yielded to Satan's temptation, the human race became infected with his moral disease. You and I tend not to notice the problem till it gets really bad—as in Auschwitz, Hiroshima, or Oklahoma City, for example. But even the smallest violation of conscience is another evidence of the problem.

Here are some questions I'd like you to think about: What should God do about this moral disease called sin? And what should He do about all the suffering it causes? Should He allow it to continue day after day, year after year, century after century? Or should He put a stop to it all?

Revelation is, above all else, a description of God's plan to put an end to sin and to restore our world to its original pristine beauty. It focuses particularly on the final phase in the conflict between good and evil.

The great white throne

Let's take a closer look at the final act in the drama; you'll find it recorded in Revelation 20:11-15. Even a casual look at this chapter makes it clear that the events in verses 10 to 15 will occur at the end of the millennium.

"Then I saw a great white throne and him who was seated on it," John says. "Earth and sky fled from his presence, and there was no place found for them" (verse 11). I doubt there's a Bible interpreter alive who would fail to recognize that the One seated on this great white throne is God Himself, the King of the universe.

There's a good reason why Revelation pictures God seated on His throne at the end of the millennium:

> I saw the dead, great and small, standing before the throne, and the books were opened. Another book was opened, which is the book of life. The dead were judged according to what they had done as recorded in the books. The sea gave up the dead that were in it, and death and Hades gave up the dead that were in them, and each person was judged according to what he had done (verses 12-14).

So this great white throne is God's *judgment* throne!

Now here's an interesting question. Why does God plan a judgment at this stage of earth's history—at the *end* of the millennium, a thousand years *after* the second coming of Christ? Wasn't the decision of who would be saved and who lost made before the millennium even began? What's the point of another judgment at the end of the millennium?

The answer, I believe, is found in Romans 14:10, 11:

> We will all stand before God's judgment seat. It is written: "As surely as I live," says the Lord, "every knee will bow before me; every tongue will confess to God."

The words "every knee will bow before me" and "every tongue will confess to God" are actually quoted from the Old Testament. They were first written by the prophet Isaiah (chapter 45:23). The way the New Testament applies Isaiah's statement makes it clear that at some point during a time of divine judgment, every human being will bow before God and confess that He is true and just.

In another place Paul expands this thought. He says that "*every* knee [will] bow, in heaven and on earth and under the earth, and *every* tongue [will] confess that Jesus Christ is Lord" (Philippians 2:10, 11).

It should be obvious to even the most casual observer that these predictions have not yet been fulfilled. Few people, of all those who have ever lived, have actually knelt before God and confessed Him as Lord. So when will all these others make this confession? While Revelation does not say so, I believe it will happen during the great-white-throne judgment at the end of the millennium.

Why the wicked kneel

Why, though? Isn't it enough that God's own people have acknowledged Him as Lord? Why is it so important that the wicked bow the knee and confess the lordship of God?

The answer to that question lies in another question: Why did God allow sin to continue these many millenniums of world history in the first place? Why didn't He just snuff Satan and the angels who followed him out of existence the moment they rebelled? Why did He allow human suffering to continue when He could have stopped it at the very beginning?

Consider the consequence to the universe had God snapped His fingers and said, "Satan, be gone!" When Satan challenged God's government (see Isaiah 14:12-14), every angel in heaven had to make a choice: Whose side would he be on? Where would his loyalty lie?

Had God eradicated the rebellion at its inception, those in the universe who had remained loyal would have seen Him as a tyrant, and they would have cowered before Him in fear. The only way God could resolve the rebellion and keep the confidence and love of His loyal supporters was to allow the rebellion to continue long enough that the entire universe could see the full outworking of Satan's plans.

Thousands of years later, at the end of the millennium, Satan's government will have reached its full maturity. Then God will be able to destroy the wicked, because the entire population of loyal beings throughout the universe, both angels and humans, will acknowledge that He is right and Satan is wrong.

At that point there will be only one group of people who still refuse to acknowledge God's supremacy and the lordship of Jesus Christ: the wicked. But when the books are opened at the great-white-throne judgment, even they will see the history of sin and rebellion from God's perspective, and even they will acknowledge the justice of God and His Son.

In a court of law, there is no better evidence in your favor than for your adversary to acknowledge that you are right. I believe that's why God thinks it important that in earth's final judgment, even His enemies acknowledge that He is right.

We still return to the question: Why is it so important that the wicked acknowledge that God is right? Because God wants to ensure that sin will never again arise in the universe. Should anyone ever *choose* to rebel again (and that possibility will always be open to every intelligent being), God would not have to run through the tragic experiment a second time. Your testimony and mine—and that of the wicked themselves at the great-white-throne judgment—will stand as evidence throughout the ceaseless ages of eternity that God is right. If there is ever another rebellion, God can safely snuff it out immediately without jeopardizing the trust that His loyal beings have placed in Him.

Judgment's terrible aftermath

Let's take one last look at the great-white-throne judgment, and especially its terrible aftermath. When that court scene has concluded and the wicked have acknowledged the justice and mercy of God, the entire universe will agree that the terrible experiment is over. Sin *must* be eradicated. Suffering *must* be brought to a close. At that time, all those whose names are not found in the Lamb's book of life will be cast into the lake of fire (see Revelation 20:14, 15).

This will be hell in its most literal sense.

Of all the pictures in the Bible, hell is the saddest, the most tragic. It's the picture of God that we least like to see, because it shows Him doing what seems so contrary to His nature—blotting humans and angels out of existence.

God sent His Son to this earth to *die* for sinners. Why is He now destroying them?

Because much as God loves sinners, He will not allow sin to remain in the universe forever. He intends to end sin's long history, with all the suffering it causes.

I don't know about you, but when that day comes, I want to be inside God's Holy City, not on the outside. I want to be on God's side, not Satan's side—because those who are on God's side will live throughout eternity in a land more beautiful than anything our minds can possibly imagine right now.

But in order to be on God's side then, we must choose to be on His side today. The last decision for God will have been made when human probation closes, shortly before the second coming of Christ.

I urge you to choose God's side today, while there is still time, before it is forever too late.

Where on Earth Is Hell?

Some people believe that hell is functioning right now and that the wicked will continue to burn alive in hell throughout the ceaseless ages of eternity. "Eternal torment," this doctrine is called. It poses several major problems. Let's look at three of them.

The most serious problem is that it turns God into a monster. Hitler, at least, was merciful enough to put his victims out of their misery. But God, we are told, will artificially sustain human beings, keeping them alive just so they can suffer throughout eternity—and all this to pay for the misdeeds of a few short years on this earth.

The second problem is that if the wicked spend eternity in hell, then evil will exist throughout eternity in at least one tiny spot in the universe. But God's plan is to eradicate sin and sinners from the universe, not to seal it off in some corner called hell (see, for example, Ezekiel 28:18, 19; Malachi 4:1-3; Revelation 21:4).

The third problem with the idea of an eternally burning hell has to do with the location of this unfortunate event. Some people claim that hell is in the center of the earth, others that it is in a distant part of the universe. But the Bible is very clear about the location of hell. Revelation 20:9 says that fire will come down from heaven *to earth* and destroy those who are in rebellion against God. Second Peter 3:10 conveys the same idea. A day is coming, it says, when "the elements will be destroyed by fire, and the earth and everything in it will be laid bare."

In other words, hell will take place on the surface of our planet.

But according to Revelation 21:1, God plans to recreate the earth, making of it a new world—restoring to it the pristine beauty that it had when He gave it to our first parents. That poses a problem to those who believe in an ever-burning hell: How can God make our world, the location of hell, into the eternal home of the redeemed if those fires continue on forever?

He can't. So, for a very practical reason it's obvious that God plans that hell will only last for a short time.

chapter fourteen

God's New World: What It Will Be Like

Some time ago, I heard the story of a missionary teacher in a tropical country who told his students that in the middle of the winter in his home country of America, water fell from the sky as ice.

The students laughed and said that would be impossible. Ice could only form in a very cold place, such as a freezer or the freezing compartment of a refrigerator—"and it never gets that cold outside." The teacher insisted that what he told them was true, but they refused to believe him.

Several years later, one of those students came to America to complete his higher education. He enrolled at a university in the northern part of the United States—and, of course, saw for himself that in the winter, water did indeed fall from the sky as ice. So he wrote back to his friends and told them that everything the teacher had said was true. But even though they were hearing it from one of their own now, they still had difficulty believing it.

Consider for a moment how *you* would describe the Antarctic to the members of a tribe deep in a tropical jungle, along the Amazon, for instance—to people who've had little or no contact with the world outside their region.

You might begin by mentioning things they were familiar with that do *not* exist in the Antarctic. For example, you might

115

point to the trees in the jungle and say, "There are no trees in the Antarctic."

Your Amazonian friends would point to a field that had been cleared of trees and ask if the Antarctic looked like that. You'd say, "Yes, only there's no grass in the Antarctic, either." Whereupon they'd point to a patch of dirt and ask if the Antarctic was all bare ground. You'd say, "There's dirt in the Antarctic, but you can't see it because it's covered with frozen water."

And that's where your explanation would have to stop—because frozen water doesn't exist in the Amazon jungle. The best you might do would be to show your jungle friends a piece of clear glass. Glass looks enough like ice that it can *represent* ice well.

Describing the new earth

Two thousand years ago, God gave His disciple John a little preview of the new earth that He plans to create someday. I'm sure that world will be as different from anything you and I have ever experienced as the Antarctic is different from the Amazon jungle. So perhaps you can understand the problem John had trying to describe the new earth to the rest of us humans who have never seen it.

Please give him credit for trying, though. He did the best he could by describing the new earth in terms of the things that you and I are familiar with. One thing he did was to tell us what the new earth *won't* be like, just as you and I might tell a group of Amazonians that there aren't any trees in the Antarctic.

John said, for example, that there will be no more death or mourning or crying or pain in God's new earth (see Revelation 21:4).

Can you imagine a land where nobody ever gets sick—no cancer, AIDS, heart attacks, or even the flu? Can you imagine a land with no hospitals, no doctors and nurses, no pharmacies, and no pills? You won't need medical insurance on the new earth or a funeral home or a cemetery.

And if there'll never be any pain, then you and I will never have to suffer through divorce. We'll never weep over sharp criticism from a person we had thought was a friend. There will be no more depression or discouragement, no mental illness to make life miserable. Psychiatrists and psychologists will be out of work on the new earth!

The New Jerusalem

Revelation says that on the new earth there will be a city called New Jerusalem. This city will have walls made of jasper, and the foundations of the walls will be made of all kinds of precious stones, including jasper, emerald, sapphire, and amethyst. And each of the city's twelve gates will be made of a single pearl!

Of course, there's always the possibility that the walls and their foundations won't be made of precious stones at all and that the gates won't really be made of pearl. Perhaps that was the closest John could come to finding something we are familiar with to describe something we've never seen.

John went on to say "the great street of the city was of pure gold, like transparent glass" (verse 21). Gold I can understand, and transparent glass I can understand. But transparent gold? There must be a reality to "Main Street" in the New Jerusalem that you and I cannot understand—something that "transparent gold" most adequately suggests.

There'll be a river in the new earth too. Revelation calls it the "river of the water of life." And it says that this river will be "as clear as crystal." It will flow from God's throne "down the middle of the great street of the city" (Revelation 22:1, 2). This description of the river sounds pretty realistic to me. Maybe this river is one of those things that will be similar enough to earthly things that we can actually understand it.

Revelation goes on to say that a "tree of life" will grow beside this river—but John's description sounds a bit odd. He says that the tree will grow "on each side of the river" (verse 2).

I've often seen trees growing along the banks of rivers, but I must admit that I've never seen a single tree growing on *both* sides of a river. Maybe the tree of life will be like that huge arch beside the Mississippi River in St. Louis, Missouri. Maybe it will have trunks that arch up from each side of the river and meet in the middle, and the branches and leaves of the tree will grow out over the river.

Something else that's different about this tree is the way it will grow its fruit. The trees we know grow one crop of fruit each year, but John says that the tree of life will bear a new crop each month (see chapter 22:2). Whether each month's fruit will be different (as some people have speculated) is unclear from John's description.

John also says that the leaves on this tree will be "for the healing of the nations" (verse 2). The Bible gives us a hint of what this might mean. In Genesis 3:22 God said that He banished Adam and Eve from the Garden of Eden to prevent them from eating of the tree of life and thus living forever. Apparently something about the tree of life will block the aging process—perhaps it offers some vitamin that we've never heard about.

Revelation also says that there will be no night on the new earth. The night we know now is caused by the rotation of our planet on its axis. At first glance it seems strange that the rotation of the new earth on its axis wouldn't create light and dark parts of the day. But John has an explanation. We won't need a sun, he says, or any artificial light such as a lamp or a flashlight, because God will give us light (see verse 5).

These are the high points of John's description of the new earth and its capital city, New Jerusalem. Yet I must tell you that I still have not shared with you the most important part of life on that recreated planet.

The best part

An atheist once said to a Christian, "What if you get to heaven and there are no pearly gates and no streets of gold?

The Christian replied, "You don't understand. Heaven isn't where there are pearly gates and streets of gold. Heaven is where Jesus is."

I like that.

At the very beginning of his description of the new earth, John says, "Now the dwelling of God is with men, and he will live with them. They will be his people, and God himself will be with them and be their God" (Revelation 21:3).

From the beginning of earth's history, God has had a deep longing to be with human beings. Let me make that more personal: *From the beginning of earth's history, God has had a deep longing to be with you and me!* Even when our first parents disobeyed Him, He came down to this earth and met with them in the garden one last time.

But God put a barrier between us humans and Himself when He cast Adam and Eve out of the garden of Eden, and for the next four thousand years no one could see Him. Then God sent Jesus—whose name, *Immanuel*, means "God with us" (Matthew 1:23)—into the world. And Jesus told His disciples that when they looked at Him, they saw God (see John 14:9).

Still, Jesus stayed on this earth only a little more than thirty years; then He returned to heaven. So again, for the past two thousand years, no one on earth has stood personally, physically, in the presence of God. We haven't been able to touch Him or converse directly with Him.

This will all change with the second coming of Jesus. At that time, He will take His people to be with Him in heaven for one thousand years.[1] During that time, we will be able to converse with Jesus and probably with God the Father as well.

But Revelation's promise that God will be "with us" comes in its description of the new earth. And it's not just that we will be able to see God occasionally. Revelation says that "the dwelling of God [will be] with men, and he will live with them" (verse 3).

Revelation says that God will live in our home and we will live in His home!

It has always been God's desire to live with us humans, whom He created in His image. I believe that for these thousands of years of earth's history He has longed to make His home with us and for us to make our home with Him. Unfortunately, sin has frustrated that plan.

But finally, in the earth made new, God's great desire will be fulfilled. We, the people He loves and who love Him, will live together with Him at last! I don't know whether God sheds tears, but if He does, then I believe when that day finally comes He will weep for joy.

Perhaps we could compare our separation from God to the separation a war brings into the lives of a young couple when one of them—let's say the husband—is a soldier. Every day the wife searches the mail for a letter from him—and how she rejoices when she finds one! Yet her life is not complete as long as he is still out on the battlefield. She never knows when she may receive a notice that says he is missing in action or, worse still, that he's been killed. But he survives the war, and the day finally arrives when he steps out of the jetway at the airport.

Do you think she will cry when she finally holds him in her arms again? Something would be wrong if she didn't!

Yes, if God weeps, then He will shed tears when He is finally able to bring His New Jerusalem and His throne down to this earth and make His home with us. God will weep when He realizes that never again will He have to wonder whether the ones He created in His image will become casualties in the war with Satan. Never again will He have to be separated from those He loves and whom He and His dear Son paid such a great price to redeem.

I believe that the war is nearly over. Yet you and I are still on that battlefield with Satan. Whether or not we become casualties in that war is up to us. It all depends on the choices we make.

Those choices will be increasingly difficult as we approach earth's final battle. We have learned in our study of Revelation that this battle is more spiritual than it is physical. The ammunition is ideas, not bullets. White-hot issues will rage in the world during its final days, and Satan will do everything he can to cloud them in mystery so that you and I will be deceived.

Increasingly, as we approach the end of time, the keys to our success in this battle will be keeping our faith in Jesus firm and determining above all else to serve and obey Him. That choice will guarantee us a place in God's new earth, a home in His New Jerusalem. And it's by choosing to trust and obey Jesus *today* that you and I can be certain that we will share eternity with Him *then*.

---

1. Heaven is a much different place from the new earth, which we have been discussing in this chapter. Chapter 11 of this book gives a more complete explanation of the second coming of Christ—at which the righteous will be taken to heaven—and chapter 12 explains the millennium—which the righteous will spend in heaven.

chapter fifteen

The End of the Journey

I like endings.

Take the end of a long journey. Back in 1993, my wife and I spent three weeks vacationing in China. The Chinese people were wonderful, the food was out of this world, and we enjoyed getting acquainted with a culture we hadn't known well before. But when our vacation time was up, it felt good to get back home!

Or think of the end of a story. Have you ever read a dramatic story or watched a dramatic motion picture? Usually there's lots of conflict and sometimes sad scenes that bring tears to your eyes. But it feels good when everything turns out right in the end.

I like endings—the end of a journey, the end of a story.

Which, I guess, is why I like this chapter. For one thing, it's the end of a long project—the last chapter in this book. But I also like this chapter because it brings us to the end of Revelation's long journey; it's the conclusion of the most dramatic story of all time. Let's take a moment to review the highlights of that journey.

Though it may not seem so at first glance, Revelation is really a story—the story of the conflict between good and evil that has been going on in our world for thousands of years. In just a few short verses, Revelation carries us clear back to the beginning of that conflict:

There was war in heaven. Michael and his angels fought against the dragon, and the dragon and his angels fought back. But he was not strong enough, and they lost their place in heaven. The great dragon was hurled down—that ancient serpent called the devil, or Satan, who leads the whole world astray. He was hurled to the earth, and his angels with him (Revelation 12:7-9).

These few brief sentences inform us that evil and suffering originated with Satan. They also give us a snapshot of how it all began: Satan was once one of God's loyal angels, but he rebelled, and God cast him onto our planet.

According to Genesis 3:1-15, shortly after Satan arrived on earth, he deceived our first parents into joining with him in his rebellion against God. From that time to the present, the human race has been involved in a life-and-death struggle between the forces of good and evil.

Satan is a very powerful, crafty enemy, and by ourselves there is no way we could ever outmaneuver him or defeat him. Fortunately, though, God didn't leave us alone in the battle against Satan. He sent Jesus to fight on our side. Of course, Satan didn't like that, and he tried to get rid of Jesus. Here's how Revelation's symbolic language tells that part of the story:

A great and wondrous sign appeared in heaven: a woman clothed with the sun, with a moon under her feet and a crown of twelve stars on her head. She was pregnant and cried out in pain as she was about to give birth. Then another sign appeared in heaven: an enormous red dragon [Satan—see verse 9] with seven heads and ten horns and seven crowns on his heads. . . . The dragon stood in front of the woman who was about to give birth, so that he might devour her child the moment it was born. She gave birth to a son, a male child, who will rule all the nations with an iron scepter (Revelation 12:1-5).

If you guessed that these verses refer to the birth of Jesus, you are absolutely right. Revelation says that the dragon—Satan—tried to destroy Jesus the moment He was born. This happened when Herod, the Roman governor of Judea at the time of Jesus' birth, ordered his soldiers to kill all the baby boys in Bethlehem up to two years of age (see Matthew 2:16).

Satan soon discovered that he could not harm Jesus. So, Revelation says, he attacked the woman who gave birth to Jesus, forcing her to flee for her life into the wilderness. We might naturally presume that this woman was Jesus' mother, Mary. However, there are several reasons why this cannot be the case.

First, nowhere does the Bible suggest that Mary was the special object of Satan's attack. Second, Revelation says that God cared for the woman in the wilderness for 1,260 days. But nowhere does the Bible say anything about Jesus' mother spending time in the wilderness. And third, a day in Bible prophecy represents a year of literal time—which in this case means the prophesied period lasts 1,260 years. But Mary, Jesus' mother, didn't live that long!

So it seems quite obvious that just as the dragon in Revelation 12 represents Satan, the woman represents something other than the person named Mary who gave birth to Jesus. Most Bible students understand this woman to represent God's people. Through these symbols, then, Revelation is telling us that Satan would persecute God's people for a long period of time—at least 1,260 years.

And, indeed, Revelation's prediction has been fulfilled. During the first 300 years of its existence, the Christian church was persecuted by the Roman government. And for hundreds of years after that, Christians themselves persecuted other Christians! People were burned at the stake, and many of those who were not killed for their faith spent long years in prison.

It was the spirit of the times. If you didn't believe the way the majority believed, the way the church in your area believed, you were a heretic and had to be punished. During most of the time in which this attitude prevailed in Europe, the dominant church was the Roman Catholic Church.[1] However, Protestantism arrived on the scene toward the end of this period, and Protestants did their share of persecuting dissenters too.

Fortunately, this way of thinking came to an end, so that for the past several hundred years the majority of people in the world have been free to worship according to the dictates of their own consciences.[2] Unfortunately, the Bible prophesies that the spirit of persecution will be revived all over the world at the very end of time, just before Jesus comes.

"The dragon was enraged at the woman," Revelation says, "and went off to make war against the rest of her offspring— those who obey God's commandments and hold to the testimony of Jesus" (Revelation 12:17). Chapter 13 describes two beast powers that will "make war against the saints" and "conquer them" and will threaten to kill those who worship in the politically incorrect way (verses 7, 15).

Some people don't like it when such unpleasant issues are raised. They'd just as soon we didn't bring them up. "Why not be positive about our faith?" they ask.

Let me share with you what Jesus told His disciples—keeping in mind that Jesus was the most positive person who ever lived on planet Earth:

"I am sending you out like sheep among wolves" (Matthew 10:17).

"A time is coming when anyone who kills you will think he is offering a service to God" (John 16:2).

"All men will hate you because of me" (Mark 13:13).

The truth is that Christianity has always been unpopular. Even in free countries like the United States and Canada, people who wouldn't think of physically harming others whose faith differs